# SOME AMERICANS

ABOUT

# QUANTUM
# BOOKS

QUANTUM, THE UNIT OF
EMITTED ENERGY. A QUANTUM
BOOK IS A SHORT STUDY
DISTINCTIVE FOR THE AUTHOR'S
ABILITY TO OFFER A RICHNESS OF
DETAIL AND INSIGHT WITHIN
ABOUT ONE HUNDRED PAGES
OF PRINT. SHORT ENOUGH TO BE
READ IN AN EVENING AND
SIGNIFICANT ENOUGH
TO BE A BOOK.

Charles Tomlinson

# Some Americans
## A Personal Record

University of California Press

*Berkeley* • *Los Angeles* • *London*

Acknowledgments are due to the editors of *Contemporary Literature,* the *Hudson Review,* and *Paideuma* for permission to reprint material that originally appeared in their pages.

University of California Press
Berkeley and Los Angeles, California

University of California Press, Ltd.
London, England

Printed in the United States of America


1   2   3   4   5   6   7   8   9

**Library of Congress Cataloging in Publication Data**

Tomlinson, Charles, 1927–
    Some Americans.

    (Quantum books)
    Includes index.
    1. Tomlinson, Charles, 1927–      —Friends and
associates.   2. Poets, American—20th century—
Biography.   I. Title.
PR6039.0349Z473        811'.54'09 [B]        80-12836
ISBN 0-520-04037-6

*To Brenda*

# Contents

# *Foreword*

In the following pages, I have tried to tell of the way certain American poets, together with a painter, helped an English poet find himself. I wanted also to convey to the reader what some of them were like as people. My first three chapters deal almost exclusively with America. In my fourth and last, where the mediating figure is Ezra Pound, Italy and America become an inextricable concern. The first chapter was written between 1976 and 1977, the second and third in 1978 and the fourth between 1978 and 1979. I am more than grateful to Hugh Kenner who suggested the making of this book.

Ozleworth Bottom
Wotton-under-Edge
1979

# 1
## *Beginnings*

A boy from the provinces, going up to read English at Cambridge in 1945, as I did, will have learned little of American poetry from his university teachers. None of them seemed to mention it. While still at grammar school, I had invested half a crown, that no longer extant coin, in a copy of the Sesame Books selection of Ezra Pound. This was published by Faber and Faber and is not to be confused with the *Selected Poems* edited by T. S. Eliot. We had been studying a book at school which purported to be *Modern Poetry*, edited by the now forgotten essayist Robert Lynd. The Pound was very different from what one found there. Puzzled, I read it through many times; tried to scan the opening lines of "E. P. Ode Pour L'Election de Son Sepulchre"; tried the same with "The River-Merchant's Wife." Evidently it couldn't be done. This was a naive discovery, no doubt. Scansion had figured prominently in one's education—in English, French, and Latin. I am grateful that it did. But here its only use was to point the difference, to suggest, with the *Mauberley* extract, that perhaps some type of syncopation was at work. What held my attention in

the book was the prosaic phraseology of poems like
"The Garden":

> And she is dying piece-meal
> > of a sort of emotional anaemia

and

> > . . . is almost afraid that I
> > will commit that indiscretion

That stress and pausing on "I" before the line break
was also arresting. As for the poem's opening, "Like a
skein of loose silk blown against a wall," nobody that
I knew of could have written more cleanly than that.
It was a sense of cleanliness in the phrasing that drew
me, still puzzled, to Canto 2, toward the end of the
book. I returned many times to

> Lithe turning of water,
> > sinews of Poseidon,
> Black azure and hyaline,
> > glass wave over Tyro.

and

> Salmon-pink wings of the fish-hawk
> > cast grey shadows in water,
> The tower like a one-eyed great goose
> > cranes up out of the olive-grove. . . .

The canto closed on the word "And. . . ." That was
also something to think about. But nobody told me
where to go next, either at school or at Cambridge. I
carried these talismanic fragments at the back of my

mind. After all, there were other things to think about—practically the whole of English literature from Chaucer to the end of the nineteenth century. I was also reading French and German.

The talismanic fragments somehow did their work, for what they had to teach survived the only other reading of an American that I accomplished in bulk at Cambridge. This was Whitman. He, along with Nietzsche, formed the style of the earliest unfortunate poems that I wrote on going down in 1948. Before that, shortly after my arrival at college in fact, I put out six shillings on a secondhand copy of Michael Roberts's *Faber Book of Modern Verse*. It was here I first encountered Gerard Manley Hopkins, and along with Hopkins the handful of imagist poems by T. E. Hulme—these seemed to have something in common with the clean surfaces of Pound, but I had no notion of the history of all that. There was also Marianne Moore and, again, I think I found the right talisman in "The Steeple-Jack." Prompted by this, my eye caught sight of a review of her work in an old copy of *The Criterion* which quoted from "The Jerboa":

> it stops its gleaning
> on little wheel castors, and makes fern-seed
> foot-prints with kangaroo speed.

"Rum stuff," said my roommate, when I showed it to him. "Pretty self-conscious, I should say." Perhaps he was right. He knew more about literature than I did at that date. I went on admiring the rhyming of light

against heavy beat, along with the perception the lines
contained, but in secret. When I came across "The
Fish" (in Anne Ridler's *Little Book of Modern Verse*), I
kept it to myself. What would he have thought of the
way that title became the subject of the first sentence
of the poem?

> *The Fish*
>
> wade
> through black jade.

No, I couldn't possibly have this doubted and discussed. I would have to explain also the appeal of the
splitting of article from noun on two occasions and in
two ways:

>       . . . the submerged shafts of the
> sun,
> split like spun
>       glass, move themselves with spotlight swiftness
>       into the crevices—
>           in and out, illuminating
> the
> turquoise sea
>       of bodies. . . .

The dividing off of parts of language, the perceptual
accuracy, the unexpected addition—"of bodies"—to
that apparently complete "turquoise sea," the deft
rhyming—these taught me more than I could yet
confess to have learned. Why, when I admired this
sort of thing, and when I was looking at Cézanne in
the Fitzwilliam Museum, did I imagine I was a

Whitmanian vitalist? The conscious mind is a shallow thing. Or rather, it is seldom conscious enough at the right moment.

The next step was Wallace Stevens. It should have been Stevens and William Carlos Williams. I will explain. I muffed the thing badly. One evening, late in 1947, my new tutor—my earlier tutor had passed me on as a hopeless case—read to me, in a pub in Trumpington, Williams's "Tract" from Oscar Williams's *Little Treasury of Modern Poetry, English and American.* I thought it delightful. He handed me the book to reread it and, as he did so, the pages fell open at Stevens's "Thirteen Ways of Looking at a Blackbird." I gazed through this rapidly then moved back to "Tract." It was "Thirteen Ways" that stayed in mind. However, as I didn't possess the anthology, and as Stevens was unpublished in England, I did not reencounter the poem for two or three years. The Williams sank from recollection. He also was unobtainable and I was not to read him seriously until 1956. And, besides, there remained that paper on Spenser to be prepared, Aristotle's *Poetics,* Book ten of Plato's *Republic* to read. The name of my new tutor was Donald Davie. At the time, I do not think he knew much more about American poetry than I did. In quantity, perhaps less. He hadn't labored through all that Whitman.

On going down from Cambridge in the summer of 1948, I found myself reading a lot of poetry I'd previously not had the time to explore. The Americans as yet were no clear enthusiasm, and poets

whom I was to find increasingly intriguing as I read
them in extenso—Moore, Stevens, and Williams—
were simply not available. These stood to one side of
the metaphysical tradition which was still very much
in the air, vouched for by Eliot and F. R. Leavis,
whereas a poet like Allen Tate could be recognizably
associated with that tradition. His selected *Poems,
1920–1945* appeared in 1947. William Empson was
also coming forward into renewed prominence and
—diverse as they were—one could read him side by
side with Tate with little sense of incongruity.

This training in the metaphysicals, whatever else it
did for one, gave little help for recognizing the kind
of thing that a Williams was after. Between 1948 and
1951 I read a lot of Augustan poetry. This provided a
good antidote to the effects of Dylan Thomas's
romanticism, for Dylan Thomas was still the voice
which sounded in one's ears as one sought for a contemporary style or, quite literally, if one switched on
the BBC. Pound and his "sinews of Poseidon" was
also an antidote, and with the publication of *The Pisan
Cantos* in 1949 a returning presence on the scene. I
also acquired, on loan, a precious copy of Miss
Moore's *Selected Poems* of 1935, and from the same
source (the poet, Ronald Bottrall) Hart Crane's 1933
*Collected Poems*. This was a book that, round about
1950, stopped me in my tracks. The sequence that laid
hold of me was not "The Bridge" (except for "Cutty
Sark," which I already knew from Roberts's anthology) but "Voyages":

Meticulous, past midnight in clear rime

—that was a voice that appealed to me, and:

The bay estuaries fleck the hard sky limits.

At the same time I recognized something else in Crane besides this sharp, perceptual view of the sea—an ache that took me back to my growing dissatisfaction with Whitman, an ache that, if I read the poems correctly, was suicidal. Of course, one had the evidence of Crane's own life. In "Voyages" itself, as in the apostrophe to the "bright striped urchins," there seemed to be a clear recognition that, with the sea,

there is a line
You must not cross nor ever trust beyond it
Spry cordage of your bodies to caresses
Too lichen-faithful from too wide a breast. . . .

Yet, at the same time, Crane yearned for a sea imagined as an experience of paradisal unity where "sleep, death, desire" merged into one as "a floating flower." As I read it then—and wrote an essay in 1950 to try to argue the matter out—Crane saw the choice as one between individual, self-responsible life and nonindividual death, and he chose the latter. He dreamed of some understanding only to be felt in "the vortex of our grave" or "the seal's wide spindrift gaze toward paradise." This paradise seemed to be reached, as in Whitman, by a surrender of self, a violation of the limits of the self, in a communion with impersonal forces, and must involve not just the death of the self, but the death of that sense of individual responsibility which conscience bids us never to violate even for the most obsessive idea or the most spiritual ideal. Besides Whitman, Crane reminded me of Emerson's "shudder of awe and delight with which the individual soul always mingles with the universal soul," and also of Poe's "Think that the sense of individual identity will be gradually merged in the general consciousness" in *Eureka,* where a pseudo-scientific vision of the universe striving back into original Oneness seemed to supply the rationalization of a wished-for psychic state. At the same time, I admired the writing of "Voyages," grudgingly, feeling a schism in the contrast of exact description or evocation (what the human eye can, humanly, see, the ear hear) and the more indefinite synaesthetic mode of apprehending things (what is felt in the process of an imagined union with nature).

The way I then read Crane was undoubtedly prompted by D. H. Lawrence's diagnosis of Whitman in *Studies in Classic American Literature,* as "always wanting to merge himself into the womb of something or other." It was that desire to merge, common also to Poe and Emerson, that seemed to be active in Crane's case. Perhaps I identified him too closely with Poe, whose *Eureka* I had just read and in which Poe's desire to merge suggested a wish to reject all personal responsibility and, simultaneously, to stand in some kind of rapport with others and with nature. Hence, conceivably, the recourse to drugs and alcohol, as in Crane's case, with the attendant feeling of release from his own ego. I had also been reading Baudelaire during this period, and a quotation from his "Of Wine and Hashish" appeared to fit Crane's "Voyages": "Il ne serait peut-être pas bon de laisser un homme en cet état au bord d'une eau limpide; comme le pêcheur de la ballade, il se laisserait peut-être entraîner par l'Ondine."

So I extrapolated my view of Crane from his poem, finding my way closer and closer to my own basic theme—that one does not need to go beyond sense experience to some mythic union, that the "I" can only be responsible in relationship and not by dissolving itself away into ecstacy or the Oversoul. Crane brought this theme to bear for me more decisively than any poet I had read before. My talismanic fragments—Pound's "lithe turning of water," Miss Moore's penetration of the sea in "The Fish" while refusing to merge with it—were also working for me; and their way of writing was working for me in its attention to word and thing.

Rereading, soon after Crane, Stevens's "Thirteen Ways"—an American friend had procured *Harmonium* for me—with its sharp, discrete fragments, I saw all at once a possibility of writing that would release me from the rather predictable stanzas that were to make up my first pamphlet, *Relations and Contraries,* in 1951. In the title of that pamphlet I already had my theme, yet perhaps only in one poem there did I start out along the path into which American writing was leading me. It began:

> Wakening with the window over fields
> To the coin-clear harness jingle as a float
> Clips by, and each succeeding hoof fall, now remote,
> Breaks clean and frost-sharp on the unstopped ear. . . .

This very English scene—yes, milk was still delivered by horse float just over twenty-five years ago—was intended as a piece of Poundian syncopation, modelled on that "Ode Pour L'Election de Son Sepulchre" which I could not scan. "The unstopped ear," quoted from the same poem's "caught in the unstopped ear," implied in my own variation that the ear was unstopped not to the sirens' song, but to the sharpness of sense experience—to the sort of sound you might hear "meticulous, past midnight in clear rime," though this was in broad day. Reading Stevens's "Thirteen Ways" led me for a while to look from different angles at separate instances of the meticulous:

> Pine-scent
> In snow-clearness
> Is not more exactly counterpointed
> Than the creak of trodden snow
> Against a flute.

This, too, was the fruit not only of reading Stevens: "pine-scent in snow clearness" had been one of my talismanic fragments for years, and if I had possessed Miss Moore's scrupulousness, it would have been printed in quotation marks. At eighteen I had seen a reproduction of a Chinese landscape with precisely that title. The two sensations, perfectly combined, perfectly separated, seemed even at eighteen to be an instance of extraordinary purity, a possibility for right feeling. Years later I recognized their implication in Pound's "radiant world where one thought cuts through another with clear edge, a world of moving energies, magnetisms that take form. . . ."

I imitated Stevens's "Thirteen Ways," but the poem I chose to write an essay on in 1951 was "The Comedian as Letter C"—another poem of the ocean, and one in which the hero Crispin suggested an alternative to Crane's mystical approach and to his sea-merge. I rather regretted the fact that, after leaving the sea a different man, Crispin came to a somewhat bourgeois Gemütlichkeit. However, he did not attempt to lose identity in the ocean, but rather to allow himself to be changed by the experience of it—to see the world afresh rather than take off into the absolute. The challenge of Crane's "Voyages" made me see how often my own preferred American poems had been sea-pieces. Pound's second Canto, Miss Moore's "The Fish," "The Steeple-Jack," "A Grave," Stevens's "Comedian," and, retrospectively, Whitman's "Sea Drift"—all these seemed to propose a moral terrain where you must confront nature, and they implied for me a moral atmosphere that itself partook of the sharpness of brine and sea breeze.

I sent my paper on "The Comedian" to Stevens as well as a commentary on his "Credences of Summer." His reply concerning the second piece appears on page 719 of *Letters of Wallace Stevens*. Acknowledging the account of "The Comedian" in an unpublished letter of July 3, 1951, he drew my attention to something I had failed to take account of and that, so far as I know, subsequent critics have also ignored:

. . . this poem exploits sounds of the letter c; hence its title. These sounds include all the hard and soft variations and pass over into other sounds, or, rather, the sound of other letters, for example in the line

> Exchequering from piebald fiscs unkeyed,

where ex contains the c sound. So, too, do ch, que, scs and k. This grows tiresome if one is too conscious of it, but it is easy to ameliorate the thing.

An odd way to write poems, I thought, but a regard for such minute particulars of language was, anyway, a healthier sign in a poet, perhaps, than the desire to lose himself in the Oversoul or spin away into "the vortex of our grave."

The fifties were an unpropitious time to write the kind of verse that interested me, and England an un-propitious place in which to publish it. An heir of Pound, Moore, Crane, Stevens must inevitably ap-pear an odd fish in English waters. I wrote the poems that comprise my short book *The Necklace* between December 1950 and March 1953. They first appeared, with a small press, in 1955 and would not have ap-peared then, had Donald Davie not contributed an in-troduction. It was Hugh Kenner's review of this booklet for *Poetry* in the summer of 1956, and the subsequent interest in what I was writing by the editor, Henry Rago, that sustained me through a state of mental emigration and led to a first visit to the United States. Simultaneously, I could also count on and received the criticism and encouragement of Donald Davie. By the date of Kenner's review in 1956 I had virtually completed a full-scale collection, *Seeing Is Believing,* adding a few more poems to the manuscript in the following year. This book found no English publisher—I tried most of them—until 1960. It was to appear in New York.

Critics have spoken of the presence of Williams in both *The Necklace* and *Seeing Is Believing,* but I did not seriously begin to read Williams until the autumn of 1956—his *Desert Music* and *Journey to Love*—and I doubt that very much could have percolated. Soon afterward I went through *Paterson,* unconvinced of its success except for certain passages. I had also been reading *Light and Dark* by that underestimated poet from upper New York State, William Bronk. It was pressed on me by Gael Turnbull, who had lent me the Williams volumes. At that period he was running Migrant Books, in Worcester, an organization for circulating recent American and Canadian works which appealed to him. From the same source I early acquired Robert Creeley's *The Whip* and his stories, *The Gold Diggers,* also the two-volume Stuttgart edition of Charles Olson's *Maximus Poems.*

The distinguishable American presences in my own work, so far as I can tell, were, up to then, Pound, Stevens, and Marianne Moore, and yet, if through them the tonality sounded American, the tradition of the work went back to Coleridge's conversation poems. At the same time, I had absorbed from Eliot's criticism what he had perhaps absorbed

from Santayana's "The Poetry of Barbarism,"
namely a suspicion of the romantic ego and of the
notion that poetry can be carried through by the gust
of personality and intensity. All this—and I shall not
tax the reader's patience much longer with the search
for "influences"—worked together with my own
painting and with the sort of visual and literary disci-
pline I had learned from passages like Ruskin's famous description of the fir tree:

The Power of the tree . . . is in the dark, flat, solid tables of
leafage, which it holds out on its strong arms, curved
slightly over them like shields, and spreading towards the
extremity like a hand. It is vain to endeavour to paint the
sharp, grassy, intricate leafage until this ruling form has
been secured; and in the boughs that approach the spectator
the foreshortening of it is just like that of a wide hill-
country, ridge just rising over ridge in successive distances.

I read this to Hugh Kenner twenty years ago, and recently (in *A Homemade World,* 1975) he has quoted
and applied it very justly to the development in modern American poetry effected by Marianne Moore. I
am certain that Miss Moore knew the passage and
that Ruskin is one of the texts that she and I had in
common.

On first meeting Kenner in England in November
1956, I was moved to learn from him that Miss
Moore had read his review of *The Necklace,* had been
interested in his quotations, and had remarked: "I
think there is as much Moore as Stevens in them." In
visiting her on his way through New York, he had

had in his possession a copy of her latest book, *Like a Bulwark,* intended for myself. When he delivered this in Somerset, it was inscribed in her hand:

> For Mr. Charles Tomlinson
> from Hugh Kenner
> and might I say? from
> Marianne Moore
> November 10, 1956

I was cheered that anyone could take an artist's position as seriously as Kenner in his generosity took mine, once I had shown him my paintings and also the new manuscript—the bulk of *Seeing Is Believing* —which I realized was certainly unpublishable in England. He even spoke of the matter to Wyndham Lewis, and reported him as saying, "Tell him by all means to go to America."

After receiving *Like a Bulwark,* I wrote almost immediately to Miss Moore, enclosing a copy of *The Necklace* and writing out for her the Victorian notice from the tower of the Clifton Camera Obscura at Bristol:

. . . the camera obscura to those unacquainted with it has a magical effect, the movement of persons, animals and carriages, the waving of foliage and the coming and going of ships being caught in the picture with the distinction and vivid colouring of nature and affording a high gratification to the observer from the continual changes and varying effects of light and shade upon the landscape.

Her reply, gratifyingly swift, was written on November 24, 1956:

Dear Mr. Tomlinson,

I thank you for your good wishes, for the Victorian notice outside the Bristol tower with a camera obscura at the
top—*indeed* a poem—and I thank you for The Necklace.
I am complimented that you think your work resembles
mine. I shall now see if I can make mine resemble yours:
i.e., The Bead, The Art of Poetry, 'the facets of copious-
ness', the sea 'rolling and unrolling fringes from sub-
merged rocks' and the 'bee's wing.'

I cannot, alas, match your address, shall have to be con-
tent with writing it.

It was a little aggressive of me to seize the opportunity
to join Hugh Kenner in giving you my book which was
*his* gift. . . .

Sincerely yours
Marianne Moore

Late in February 1957 I wrote my first poems in
emulation of the three-ply cadences that Williams
used in the two books of his I had read. I completed,
to begin with, "Sea Poem," "Winter," "Le Musée
Imaginaire," and "Letter to Dr. Williams." Shortly
afterward I made an exchange with Hugh Kenner—
in return for the correspondence of Hilaire Belloc, he
sent me Williams's *Collected Earlier Poems* and *Collected Later Poems.* For the time being, however, it was
the three-ply poems that appealed to me most,
perhaps because they afforded the possibility of a
more meditative movement. They served also later
on when, with the help of Henry Gifford, I came to
translate Antonio Machado and needed a form that
would progress at a speed resembling that of thought,

while avoiding the rather facile rattle that occurs if one translates Spanish octosyllabics directly into English with end rhymes.

When I began imitating Williams's measure and applying it to the cadences of an Englishman's English, I was still finding it difficult to place poems in my native country and this new, apparently odd layout was hardly going to be a recommendation in the eyes of editors. A number of my things had found a home for themselves in *Spectrum,* a little magazine published by students at the University of California at Santa Barbara. Hugh Kenner served on the advisory board and, in 1957 when he was teaching at Santa Barbara, so did Donald Davie. I sent "Letter to Dr. Williams" to *Spectrum,* and it came out in the autumn number, 1957, immediately following a poem of Williams's own. Seeing them together, I wrote to Williams to establish contact.

In the meantime, thanks once more to Hugh Kenner, the much refused manuscript of *Seeing Is Believing* had gone off to a new publishing house in New York, McDowell Obolensky. On Christmas Day 1957 two things occurred: I received news of their acceptance of the book and also a postcard from Williams promising a letter "in reply to your poem in *Spectrum*" and ending, "Take care of yourself. Poetry is a tough racket." A few days later the letter arrived:

Dear Tomlinson:

Through Hugh Kenner I have just become acquainted with your name, God be praised! for to meet an Englishman to whom my name is not anathema is almost to be classed by me as an event. Not that I give a damn except as it signalizes the advent of someone who may turn out to be a friend.

That poem which has been printed in *Spectrum* seems to clinch the matter. What you have written in that poem is high praise for me and I am all the more impressed that you have allowed yourself to copy (in this instance) my form. Anyone who is influenced by a verse form which liberates English verse is my friend.

Let's not go into that at the moment. I am amazed that your lines fall so easily and beautifully into the pattern of my verses in Desert Music and Journey to Love. It makes me feel that my deviations are valid and not mere eccentricities—and that they may be susceptible of proliferation. There is no room for rancour in any serious study of English verse, your attitude shows a light hearted spirit which is tremendously encouraging to me. As you may know I have not many friends among the scholars in this country as well as England. A small clan makes for penetration in the attack when our front must be consolidated at all costs. . . .

It was encouraging for me in return to find myself so suddenly one of a clan whereas previously my sense had been of almost complete poetic isolation. A new clan had also been preparing itself in England— this was the group of poets known as the Movement. I shared their feelings about the need to displace the last of the forties neoromanticism and the uncritical admiration for Dylan Thomas, yet I felt the whiff of little Englandism in their manifestoes and in some of their verse to be a symptom of that suffocation which has affected so much English art ever since the death of Byron. Though Davie rode with the Movement, their ranks and their anthologies were closed against my own work. He, too, curiously enough, was producing poems at the time influenced strongly by an American model—namely, the verse of Yvor Winters. But Winters was more easily assimilable among English notions—after all he wrote in quatrains— than was my own choice of American poets. That Davie was a Poundian—though not noticeably in his verse as yet—was to lead him eventually to an interesting and fruitful state of literary schizophrenia.

With the Movement then at large in England, to be admitted into Williams's clan lent me a renewed sense of confidence. Perhaps this was slightly unreal, for the main body of the work I had already accomplished had very little to do with Williamsite procedures, though I could see that it intersected at certain points with his concerns. Williams, after all, had to face out a sense of cultural deprivation and overcome alienating forces very different from the day-to-day experiences of a European. When Kenner says that his chief technical discovery was "that words set in Jersey speech rhythms say less but mean it with greater finality," he makes a valuable formulation. But that is hardly a task to which a European could pretend to address himself.

In listening to Jersey speech rhythms and to what he calls "the American language," Williams evolved his theory of "measure." "Measure"—by which I take him to mean those structural principles that still

subsist in the language of poetry when one has abandoned traditional metrics—he seems to have supposed, in his more polemical moments, belonged to a
specifically American poetry. Already I was trying to
prove that "measure" belonged also to English
poetry, though I would have hesitated to define it in
terms of Williams's variable foot, that self-contra-
dictory notion which Alan Stephens parodies in the
phrase "an elastic inch." Yet to be admitted to the
clan, on whatever grounds, was an honor, for I felt
it to be a platoon in a much larger action, one that
would eventually establish the importance of other
American poets in England besides T. S. Eliot.

Once I had heard from Williams, I sent to him "Sea
Poem," which struck me as superior to the verse letter. He replied in the New Year:

Dear Charles:

   'Sea Poem' is a fine piece that impresses me both for its
scholarly composition in the English sense of the term and
for its generosity toward the American idiom and all it im-
plies for me. . . .

Did he mean by "its generosity toward the American
idiom," I asked myself, that he took me to be writing
in some sort of American? After all, if I was being
generous at all, it was toward his three-ply measure
rather than any specific idiom. My idiom was Queen's
English, deriving of course, in its poetic structure,
from an American example. But "American idiom"?
I feared that when McDowell Obolensky brought
out *Seeing Is Believing* in the summer of 1958, he

would find it uninteresting, because if he read it in the light of its influences, they were clearly pre-Williams and the themes of a decidedly English and European cast.

On this score I was wrong. His enthusiasm for the book brought an immediate letter on its publication and eventually a review in the pages of *Spectrum*. I shall not quote Williams's letter or review in detail since they are mostly adulatory of my own work and, while adulation may sound sweet to the recipient, it is apt to be a bore to any second party. There is *some* adulation in what I shall summarize, but the point that it goes to prove concerns Williams as much as, and perhaps more than, myself. Williams, in his mid-seventies, needed the sense of a clan. He still felt the uphill grind toward reputation in America and was not to find an English publisher till after his death. As late as 1959 the *Times Literary Supplement* for November 6 listed Williams among a heterogeneous "profusion of talents as yet unnoticed." But in another article in the same number, one read: "We have passed the period of aggressive nativeness in American poetry, the sort of thing illustrated so determinedly (and for British readers so bewilderingly) in the poetry of William Carlos Williams." Williams's aggressiveness, his anti-colonialism, was born of frustration rather than a mindless dislike of England. Indeed, he felt that the British outlook was more civilized, better informed than the American and that the British *ought* to have seen what he was up to and what measure was all about. There exists a certain

pathos in this attitude as it shows itself in a letter he
sent to Kenner on the publication of *Seeing Is Believing:* "The new world writer," he says, "can now look
up to his more cultured brother with complete trust
in him." Kenner had told him of my struggles to get
the book into print, and in this he saw not only a
reflection of his own long fight but felt, now the
book's existence was a palpable fact, that the battle for
measure had been carried into England and by an English writer. Both these things—his own remembered frustrations and an Englishman's poems with
an American flavor—caused him to describe *Seeing Is
Believing* as "the most moving book out of England
that I have ever read," "a major event in my modern
world" (letter of July 12, 1958); and later on he wrote:
"What you are doing with the poetic line . . . is a fun-
damentally important labor in the development of
English prosody." His old-fashioned sense of what
England stood for led him to write as follows in the
review:

An Englishman, if he is the guardian of his country's scholarship through an enviable tradition, cannot avoid the issue
but with the grim determination of the breed must follow
where his betters have led him. If scholarship has led him
astray he must reexamine his sources and finding an error
correct it.

That was what he took me to be doing, in this collection of poems for which he felt such delight, animated
also no doubt by his earlier pleasure at those three-ply

verses of mine where his own existence was directly saluted by an Englishman.

In 1959 I was awarded, along with six other European writers, a travel grant to visit the United States. I had been sponsored by Henry Rago of *Poetry,* but heard that Williams and Miss Moore had both written letters of recommendation. My first disappointment on getting to New York, in October 1959, concerned the fact that Marianne Moore could not be visited. She was about to go away, "so cannot," as she wrote, "seem as cordial as I feel. When I have come back, I shall ask if you might then be able to find a time for us to meet. I hope that you are not dismayed by the clatter and noise of New York, or worn out by the journey and the effort of leaving home." There was opportunity, however, for a telephone call, and I heard for the first time that voice of which Louis Zukofsky was later to say to me: "She talked like a sewing machine. You could almost count the syllables." It was an unkind, but not inaccurate, description of her curiously staccato way of speaking while emphasizing certain words. She reverted at once to her theme of the unattractiveness of New York. "This Sodom and Gomorrah of a city," she called it. "Chicago is worse," she added, "though there's a fascinating Museum of Science and Invention there. But if you say, 'I want to go to the Museum of Science and Invention,' *they* say, 'Not time.' Here, it's impossible to look around and *not* notice something unsightly. Why, to find *beauty,* Mr. Tomlinson, I had to go as far as British Columbia last summer and I found out about *that* because of a picture in the *Illustrated London News.*"

Miss Moore was leaving town for Pennsylvania to recuperate from what she described as "a near stroke." William Carlos Williams, disabled by strokes that had been more than "near," could at any rate be seen at Rutherford. Denise Levertov first took me out there to visit him. We would go after lunch, she said. That was the best time and when his mind showed itself most active. Denise was very properly and protectively solicitous for Williams. It would be preferable if my wife and child did not accompany us, for he tired easily. I assured her that the child was most biddable, a product of Europe like herself. But she remained firm—no doubt rightly so—and anyway, I was joking rather than insisting.

We lunched at Denise's apartment on West 15th Street, went by subway to the Port Authority bus station and, for the first time, I crossed that marshy flatland, the Meadows, between New York and Rutherford. Trucks were dumping their fill in the remaining spaces between suburban outcrops. Development was going forward here and there with no distinguishable center or direction. A touch of civility in the white Lutheran church whose scrupulously painted wooden structure dominated one settlement. Then: scattered filling stations, motels, wires, roads, presaging a future, perhaps. Suddenly a river with birds on it, a lost pastoral almost side by side with all this. The tree-lined back streets and the neat, wooden houses of Rutherford came as a surprise. So did the squat church that was built of a durable-looking stone.

"Wherever's your wife?" was the first thing Williams asked, turning to me, after giving Denise a forceful kiss. "And the child?" This was a good day. Despite his trailing arm, despite the occasional difficulty he had in finding words, which Mrs. Williams would supply, he seemed boyishly energetic, even radiant in his eagerness to convey in the flesh that friendship he had already offered in his letters. Both he and his wife moved in their talk between past and present. "When we came here," he said, "the place was surrounded by woods, and now—." "One thing I *would* like," said Mrs. Williams, "is to see a horse-drawn carriage or two back."

I admired their two plant pictures by Charles Demuth. "There's something else I wanted you to see," said Williams and, taking me by the arm, he propelled me upstairs. It was his workroom he wished to display: the desk, the electric typewriter, the papers, the books. What caught my eye, as we stood talking, was a metal letter-clip—Victorian I supposed—in the form of a hand, with long fingers, extending from a cuff, the metal simulating lace here, with a texture of dotted lines, circles, and zigzags. "In forty years," said Williams, "you are the only person ever to have admired that. Look, you're going to cross the continent. When you pass through New York on your way home come and see me, with your wife and child

this time, and it's yours. You have a right to it." I
feared I had all too little right to it, that I must merely
have sounded covetous.

Returning with Denise down Rutherford's main
street to the bus, I could now complete for myself
Williams's unfinished sentence about the once sur-
rounding woods. The neons were splashing and trick-
ling their colors over wet sidewalks between buildings whose graceless monotony was made drabber
and lonelier by the damp dusk of late autumn.

Three weeks had gone by when we found ourselves, on a Saturday evening, in the Lowells' car,
driving through Boston in search of a parking lot.
"Two things out of many things," Lowell's wife,
Elizabeth Hardwick, was saying, "have brought on
the lacks of the last fifteen years—the motor craze and
the school laze-craze." "Look," said Lowell—we
were driving along the bank of the neoned Charles
River—"that's just about the vista commanded from
Olive Chancellor's window in *The Bostonians.*" Yes,
James had foretold it all with his "desolate suburban
horizons, peeled and made bald by the rigour of the
season." When I next turned up a copy of *The Bostonians,* what struck me about the description of the
vista to which Lowell had referred, was how close it
stood to being a poem by Williams: "There was
something inexorable in the poverty of the scene,
shameful in the meanness of its details ... loose
fences, vacant lots, mounds of refuse, yards bestrewn
with iron pipes, telegraph poles and bare wooden
backs of places." James one would imagine to be an

antithetical writer to Williams. Yet some of the urban poetry James catches out of the corner of his eye, as it were, often contains the kind of detail out of which Williams would construct an entire poem. I am thinking of chapter fifteen of *Portrait of a Lady:* September quiet in a London square, two small children, rusty railings, a dominant red pillar box; or again, in *The Ambassadors,* book seven, chapter two: evening over Paris, a whiff of violets, "a far off hum, a sharp near click on the asphalt." Williams would have made a choreographic poem out of these details, "drawing . . . many broken things into a dance by giving them thus a full being."

Williams was often to come to mind in a journey across America that lasted some five months. In the curious cross-ply of circumstance his name was intricated, for me, with that of another antithetical figure, the poet and critic Yvor Winters. In that same number of *Spectrum* in which Williams's "Translation from Sappho" appeared side by side with my own "Letter to Dr. Williams" was Donald Davie's article, "An Alternative to Pound?" It opened as follows:

The Stanford school of poets, grouped around and schooled by Yvor Winters, seems to me perhaps the most interesting feature of the poetic scene in the U.S. Where other masters—British as well as American—have tried to come to terms with the challenge of the Poundian-Eliotic poetic mostly by diluting, muffling, taking what they want and evading the harder truths, Winters has met the challenge by offering a considered and coherent alternative, an alternative poetic theory grounded in an alternative moral-ity driving through to an alternative practice. And so, while more talent can and does spring up in other quarters of the poetic scene, it is only from the Poundian wing (and by that I mean rather Charles Tomlinson, say, than Louis Zukofsky) or else from this other extreme at Stanford, that one can expect talent, when it appears, not to have to save itself by *ad hoc* improvisations, hairsbreadth escapes and eleventh-hour expedients. It is especially good, if also ironical, that this most traditional and forbiddingly "classical" of current schools should be, at Palo Alto, within the orbit of that San Francisco bohemianism which, in its naive reliance on the generous impulse, spells death to any poetic whatever.*

"From the Poundian wing. . . ." Did that mean also Williams? For me, by that time, it must do. At all events, having read Winters and finding Davie's formulation challenging, it seemed absurd to be in California, as we were in the December of 1959, and not to visit the poet at Palo Alto. At some time between his article of 1957 and our advent, Davie, while teaching in California, had shown Winters my poem on John Constable. "Too concrete," had been the comment. But, then, one heard he had said the same to an admirer of his own poem, " A View of Pasadena from the Hills." A visit seemed worth the risk.

The preliminaries proved more bracing than ominous. I explained to Winters, over the phone, that we did not wish to trespass on his day unduly, or to put out his wife by arriving at their mealtime. "My

---

*Donald Davie, "An Alternative to Pound?" *Spectrum* 1 (Fall 1957): 60–63.

wife?" said Winters. The tone was matter-of-fact rather than surly. "I am perfectly capable of preparing you a meal myself." So, beginning with lunch at Palo Alto it was to be a whole day.

I had never before driven on an American freeway—and in the England of 1959 freeways did not as yet exist. In a borrowed car, we therefore departed early from Berkeley, determined to arrive on time. The route was unexpectedly simple and Winters's directions turned out to be lucidity itself. You cannot kill time on a freeway and once you are off it, though you fear you may now mistake the road and go astray, it is also possible to arrive at your destination with surprising speed. This we did. We were an hour early.

A tall hedge concealed the Winters's house, equally impenetrable (or so we told ourselves) from either side. We determined to sit out the hour, quietly, under its protection. Almost as soon as we drew up, Winters had appeared at the gate and was striding toward the car. My wife, the first to gather herself together, fell rather than stepped out onto the ground, apologizing, as she did so, for being late. The day had begun and would evidently end in fiasco.

However, this reputedly unaccommodating man who, it was said, could resist all attempts at conversation with a yes as curt as his no, either took pity on us or simply liked us. We did not speak much of literature, but when we did it was then that constraint entered in. Williams? He has become unreadable. Pound? A complete barbarian. The only poets Win-

ters was prepared to discuss with approval were, all
too predictably, those of his own school—Alan
Stephens, Edgar Bowers, J. V. Cunningham. Yet the
striking thing about Winters's conversation that day
was its lack of precisely that quality of ratiocinative
abstraction which he professed to admire in poetry.
His talk consisted of a celebration of the concrete:
Californian wines, Californian trees and the shapes of
their leaves, local topography and the changes the vi-
cinity had undergone, the habits of airedales, the mi-
gration of birds, the kinds of birds that visited Palo
Alto, the distinguishing peculiarities of the older Californian culture.

Later on, in his study, while preparing to sign a
copy of his *Collected Poems,* he handed to me J. V.
Cunningham's most recent book. I turned the pages
for a few moments, then saw that he was looking at
me. "Well, what do you think of *that?*" I paused before speaking. Did he really expect an instant judg-
ment? All that I could summon up was: "It looks—
er—more original than *The Helmsman.*" "Original?"
said Winters; "there is no particular virtue in original-
ity, you know." One could imagine a tone in which
that could have sounded crushing, yet it was offered
not coldly but rather as advice, something to be pondered. I hesitated to subject this gift to the argument it
invited, for, after all, it was being made simultaneously with that of his own poems. What formulated
itself in the mind, without ever reaching the tongue,
was something like, "There *are* certain obviousnesses
of tune and movement, too smoothly homing rhyme

sounds, which suggest a merely passive echoing of
traditional forms and. . . ." The thought, however,
was prompted less by any immediate consideration of
Cunningham, than by a weakness that I had always
felt marred a number of Winters's own poems, along
with certain quaint inaptnesses of diction. Here was a
poet, all rigor and closed forms, who could yet describe a military rifle as "with carven stock unbroke,"
an attempt at archaism as ungainly as (of the same
rifle) "your bolt is smooth with charm" was insi-
pidly lax.

The day was an entire success. The dignity and di-
mension of the man unmistakably communicated
themselves, as did a capacity for friendship, rather
than friendliness. Winters showed no desire to please,
but, as in his urging one to try a particularly fine
wine, he was eager to share what he deemed best. The
same eagerness appeared when he offered for one's
meditation, as it were, his distinctive vision of things
Californian. That vision was, further, tinged with a
kind of elegiac sadness, as in his poem "California
Oaks," an awareness that the place had changed and
was changing now beyond all recognition. Like
Williams, he complained: "When we first came here,
this was the country."

I was never to see Winters again, yet I have often
had cause to think of his tie with another part of
America. In northern New Mexico, there is a ghost
town called Madrid—the first syllable of the word
takes the accent. The coal mine, the town's sole *raison
d'être,* had closed long ago round about Christmas

and, for many years, the desert dryness preserved the Christmas decorations intact, including a life-size but faceless Joseph accompanying a Mary, whose features the sun had similarly obliterated, with the Christ child on an ass. On the further side of the town, the school still remains, locked and empty, its walls fissuring apart. It was here that Yvor Winters taught, after spending three years bedridden with tuberculosis in Santa Fe.

New Mexico, Atlanta, the Deep South, Baltimore, Washington, and at last, by April, New York once again. Miss Moore was now home, I imagined, and having written to her ahead from Washington, received the reply: "Monday afternoon the 25th Mr. Tomlinson? about half past 3? I was dejected thinking I had missed you. Am just making a train, —not very ceremonious." On April 23 a second note arrived:

Would it tax you too much to come to see me Monday morning the 25th about eleven or quarter of eleven? —talk for half an hour or longer; and at about twelve go with me to a small restaurant nearby for lunch—(a reliable little place, —though far from peaceful or spacious.) So please pardon that.

I do wish on *no account* to miss meeting you having managed so badly as to have been disabled for more than a month, —with deferred promises now multiplied and tasks which are *said* to be peremptory, crowding me uncivilly—I find Monday morning the most leisurely of any day afterward, until you would be leaving New York. Evenings are not so good for visiting. . . . I seem toward evening to have a froglike croak, and other vestiges of the fever and laryngitis I have suffered the past month.

(I am not contagious or physiologically a menace, however, I am glad to say). . . .

Indeed, Monday morning, it was her vivacity and not her laryngitis which proved contagious. It was an intermittent vivacity that had to struggle against the lingering effects of illness and the increasing debility of old age. At times, her face seemed completely and fadedly inert, as if all energy had far withdrawn from it. Then a smile would transform her frailty and she was back in the current of life. I have never visited her part of Brooklyn since that morning in April 1960, and have often wondered whether the wood-fronted houses there, and the houses with colonnaded balconies, have survived. The apartment building at 260 Cumberland Street was stone-faced with a massively heavy front door. Miss Moore lived five floors up in pleasantly cluttered quarters. Among the pictures were three reproductions of works by Blake, Dürer's rhinoceros, a photograph of T. S. Eliot as a boy and, beneath these, myriads of animals, including a ceramic leopard and an elephant, and a wooden alligator paper-knife, a work of therapy by a mental patient. To add to these, I gave her a small black turtle modelled in the New Mexican pueblo of Santa Clara.

For some reason—perhaps because I had written of him and she had quoted him in "An Octopus"—Ruskin was the writer of whom we spoke most. "He knew everything, didn't he!" she said. She recalled going as a young woman with her mother to see Ruskin's house at Coniston, her mind's eye still retaining the memory of a peacock's feather he had

owned and of a watercolor of the Tyrol he had
painted. I thought immediately of "The Steeple-Jack"
and "as Dürer changed / the pine tree of the Tyrol to
peacock blue . . . ," wondering whether the memory
had also reinforced the writing of that. "There is a
lovely portrait of Ruskin," she was saying. "I think
it's in Millais's *Memories.* Ruskin is the man who has
said it all. Let's see if we can find that book." We
searched, fruitlessly as it turned out, among many
dusty volumes while she aired her literary likes and
prejudices: "I never did care much for Mallarmé. . . .
Samuel Beckett? There's nothing to *find* in Samuel
Beckett. . . . *Time* magazine? I really abominate the
existence of *Time* magazine for betraying my where-
abouts. I telephoned directions on how to find this
house to their interviewer, and when the interview
appeared they printed the directions too. Since then
I've been haunted by school children demanding information. And look at this mimeographed sheet!" It
was a poem headed, "This is better than you can do,
Miss Moore." "Now, Mr. Tomlinson, have you kept
perfectly *well* during this lengthy journey of yours?"
The question was asked with such suddenness, so in-
tently and intensely, that I heard myself replying,
very much to my own horror and against my will,
that I had had dental troubles. Perhaps it was not entirely her solicitude, but also the fact that I was suffering at the very moment from toothache, that forced
the answer out of me. "Then, Mr. Tomlinson," she
returned, "I shall give you thirty dollars. I know what
our dentists are like." I assured her that there was no

need to do that, I should soon be home where things were cheaper. "I shall send it anyway," she replied; "I am sure it hasn't been cheap for you and Mrs. Tomlinson to cross this continent." I was relieved when our talk turned back to poetry. She explained to me, in great detail, which of my poems she liked—these included the Ruskin piece. "You can bring them to a conclusion without forcing it—that has always been my problem. And so I cut relentlessly." This seemed the opportunity to mention something I had long had on my mind. "I was surprised," I said, "having known 'The Steeple-Jack' for so long, to find the flower passage missing from the 1951 *Collected Poems*." She looked at me almost guiltily: "Then I may put it back," she blurted; "I get embarrassed about my own digressions and I probably cut too drastically. Yes, I may well put it back." When *A Marianne Moore Reader* appeared the following year, "The Steeple-Jack" was the first poem to appear, as in the 1951 *Collected*. This time the poem bore the subheading "Revised 1961." The flower passage had returned and in a far more extended form than that which I remembered from *The Faber Book of Modern Verse*. Five more lines of flowers had been inserted with some tinkering to follow, to tie them in.

The little restaurant was not, as she said, spacious, but it turned out to be peaceful. She was recognized at once, as how could she not be in one of her broad-brimmed hats among that soberly dressed clientele? When I left her back at her apartment, I received a subway token, as did all visitors from Manhattan,

out of a bowl of tokens, to pay my way back to town
from the Lafayette Avenue station. She asked me, as I
was leaving, if I had enjoyed New York. When I replied that I had, her face kindled with a smile that
seemed unexpectedly like gratitude: "I was afraid you
wouldn't like it—it's gotten so ugly. As for England—I could sing the praises of England from now
until doomsday."

In the middle of the week a card arrived at the Van
Rensselaer where we were staying—the grand name
though not the grand place. It stated:

The picture of Ruskin is in J. Ernest Pythian's *Pre-
Raphaelite Brotherhood* (F. Warne) by Sir John Millais; and
Ruskin is *alone* not with anyone—standing by a torrent
with one foot on a bowlder [*sic*]—and might have been
about twenty five or thirty years old.

(I had the book away at the top of a recently acquired
bookcase in the dining room.)

The turtle is one of my most precious mascots. I think
I'll call it for my brother.

Before leaving New York, I took the bus out to
Rutherford once more, accompanied by my wife and
Justine. It was shortly after Easter, and the tractable
European child played with the chickens that had
been the decoration on a now-eaten Easter cake.
These she was to carry back over the Atlantic.
Williams, for all his ills, exuded a sort of holiday gai-
ety. He told how he had once thought he might have
married the poet Mina Loy. Mrs. Williams, unim-
pressed with this item of news whether real or fic-

tional, replied drily: "She wouldn't have taken you. You didn't have enough money."

That evening, I found myself once more in Williams's workroom upstairs. "Well," he said, "here's your letter-clip." And he presented me with the Victorian metal hand reaching out of its elegantly turned lace cuff. I hardly deserved the gift. After five months travel I had completely forgotten it. When I had been in Rutherford before, I had imagined *he* would forget it. But here was the old poet, broken by strokes, whose memory had served him better than mine had served me.

Our last meeting took place that day. Williams wrote soon after our return in reply to a letter of my own:

Your view of your delapidated garden is entrancing if sad but not irretrievable after hard work—came just at the time I was heartbroken at the failure to take away the trash from our curb during our trash removal week. They did finally come just in the nick of time but the men did a very slovenly job of it. The only good work is left for our artists to do. . . . The artist must be a good craftsman which no one among the plumbers and carpenters it seems is today. Maybe we're too impatient, maybe it has always been the same.

I'm glad you found something on which to let yourself go in America even if you had to go back to the primitive Indians of the canyons to find it—Mesa Verde fascinated me too though I did not see the dances as you did.

The letter closed with enquiries after the rest of the

family, ending: "The Easter Chickens weren't seasick were they?"

We continued to exchange letters. One from Williams in December 1960 contained the following:

Certainly I know that it is winter and that is a season inimical to me. It is always unpleasant from December through March, the only thing I ever heard cheerful about it was my mother in law's annual prediction for New Year's Day, January first, now it's Spring!

It was after a silence of over a year that I received a short note in January 1962. It said simply:

Dear Charles:

I have been ill for over a year and unable to communicate with you. I picked up an old copy of the magazine Poetry and stumbled on a poem that you had written. It had a familiar ring, called to mind something over which we had been working together.

It's a theme familiar to me which we had not worked out by half. Go on developing the theme for there is much good grist still in it.

Hope you can make something out of this.

Affectionately
Bill

I never discovered what poem it was he had stumbled on. He lasted through that winter, but died the following year in March, the month when his winter thoughts had usually reached their crisis and the poems were stirring towards hope. He died just too early for us to meet when, after a second spell in New

Mexico, I returned through New York that summer.

Miss Moore—or Marianne M., as she had signed her note on Ruskin—survived him by nine years. I had written to her from Taos in the June of 1963. Alas, she was to be away on our return East, in Connecticut and then in Maine, but she replied warmly:

The Taos turtle reminds me of you daily; and I wish I might see the children and Mrs. Tomlinson. . . . We depend on you, and read you with such pleasure in POETRY. I value your caring about my changed text—of the Steeplejack.

We were, however, to meet again before her death—twice, in fact. In April 1966 I did a reading tour of New York State, accompanied by my wife, for the Academy of American Poets. A reception was arranged by my publishers at the Oxford Press. At George Oppen's place where we were staying, a letter awaited us from Miss Moore, telling of her move up to 35 West 9th Street. Not only were we to go and see her, but she would be present at the reception. A second message arrived a week later, specifying Sunday May 1st for our meeting. I noticed that the address label she had pasted over her old letterhead bore her name and middle initial for the first time—"Marianne C. Moore"—*C* for Craig.

When we arrived at Oxford with George and Mary Oppen on the afternoon of the reception, no one else had turned up as yet, or, at least, my immediate impression was that no one had. Then, on the far side of the large room, I suddenly caught sight of Miss

Moore sitting alone in a small recess, utterly still and
utterly silent. I thought at first she had gone blind, for
she had that look of blank withdrawal that one sees
sometimes on the faces of the blind. Afterwards, I
realized that her expression represented only an inten-
sification of that strange look of inertia I had noticed
when I first met her six years before. Six years had
aged her into a frailer, smaller, more helpless old lady.
What was startling was the thought that she had
crossed Manhattan on her own to come to this gathering. She was as old as Williams had been in the year of
his death, seventy-nine. Glancing at her from time to
time during the course of the reception, I often feared
that her frailty could never withstand so much bois-
terousness and I knew that the sight of so much liquor
could have been no pleasure to her. "This drinking!"
as she was to say at the tea party in her new flat;
"They even do it at Bryn Mawr now, I hear."

At the tea party she was more herself, fragile but
unexpectedly light-hearted and mercurial, in her neat
white dress dotted with blue. The presence of her
niece, Sally Moore, a capable and kind young woman, evidently set her at her ease. Her ease also meant
that she could air her opinions. She was speaking of what she called the size of poetry. "And by
poetry," she added, "I mean 'La Vita Nuova' and
'The Divine Comedy.' We don't come that big these
days, as Mr. Blackmur says." For some reason or
other she had taken a great dislike to the English critic
A. Alvarez. I am not sure whether her contempt for
him was greater or less than her contempt for

Robbe-Grillet. "Mr. Alvarez," she said, "is a snake in the grass, but the practitioners of the new French novel are idiots—simply idiots." I ventured a few diplomatic words in mild defense. She sniffed and said tartly: "You make every allowance." The point of her dislikes was that she conceived "these people" lacked "seemliness" in what they wrote. Seemliness for her had become almost a war cry, and she held forth with a puritan energy on the subject in that high room with the grimy cowls of the ventilator shafts revolving outside the window on the roof below. "William Carlos Williams often lacked it, you know. He once gave a reading of an unfortunate passage from his poems here in New York. There were two ladies in the audience who were clearly shocked by it. So I went up to them afterward and said to them: 'He isn't *always* like that.' "

We added a Mexican toad—a seemly toad carved in onyx—to the animal collection and it took up residence beside the pottery turtle. Leaving the apartment, I caught sight once more of a photograph that had arrested my attention in Cumberland Street— that of T. S. Eliot as a boy, the man clearly distinguishable in those features, which also possessed an unlooked-for insouciance that years of suffering were to veil and transform.

When *The Complete Poems of Marianne Moore* appeared in 1967, the book opened at those exemplary verses, "Poetry." They had been cut back from twenty-nine to three lines—the first of these shortened by ten words—though the original version was

printed in the notes at the end. I turned anxiously to
"The Steeple-Jack." The tinkerings of six years before had been allowed to stand as had the information
"Revised 1961," though minor changes had crept in
since then. I may have been responsible for second
thoughts in 1961, but I regret the addition of "The
climate / is not right for banyans" in place of the more
direct, "There are no banyans. . . ." And also the coy
"if you see fit" after "snake-skin ["snakeskin," as it
reads in 1967] for the foot." No, I prefer the poem as I
first read it in *The Faber Book* when, on a day thirty
years ago, I realized there was a kind of probity possible in verse for which seemliness would be no bad
description.

Moore, Williams, Winters, and Henry Rago are all
dead. They cemented a bond of affection for America
I could never have anticipated at the time of my earliest poems or of *The Necklace*. Wyndham Lewis's
"tell him by all means to go to America" has often
reechoed in the memory. My teacher and friend
Donald Davie was to follow that course in the mid-
sixties, and I have several times contemplated it myself. Time, however, has removed the temptation
while perhaps increasing the reasons for it. I have visited the States three times since the stay of 1962–63;
with that stay begins a new phase of literary relations.
For in the spring of 1963, in Albuquerque, looking
disconsolately through a pile of poetry books I had to
review for the *University of New Mexico Quarterly*, I
suddenly came upon George Oppen's *The Materials*,

and as I read these poems the weight lifted. That same spring I also met Robert Creeley for the first time and in the summer Louis Zukofsky and George Oppen himself. But this phase requires a new chapter to itself.

# 2
# *Objectivists: Zukofsky and Oppen*

"It pays to see even only a little of a man of genius."
Thus Henry James, of Flaubert. I saw Louis Zukofsky
four times, corresponded with him—on and off—
for seven years, and edited in 1964 what was,
I suppose, one of the earliest Zukofsky numbers
of an English review for *Agenda:* I was by no means
the first islander to discover Zukofsky—Ian Hamilton Finlay had brought out over here *16 Once Published* in 1962 and that had given one something to
think about. Indeed, those sixteen poems promised a
way in, whereas the translations from Catullus and
the sections of *"A"* I had already seen in *Origin* had
left me more puzzled than enlightened. Gael Turnbull, who early on had confronted me with Williams,
Creeley, and Olson, was also puzzled, though he
spoke of Zukofsky the man and also of the holy trin-
ity, Louis, Celia, and son Paul, in a way to arouse
curiosity. In 1961 Robert Duncan's poem "After
Reading 'Barely and Widely'" had caught one's eye
in the *Opening of the Field*—

will you give yourself airs
from that lute of Zukofsky?

But the book was simply not available on which to
judge that lute, and it was not until August 1963 that I
came to own No. 132 of the three hundred copies in
which edition "Barely and Widely" was printed—in
a facsimile of Louis Zukofsky's handwriting and published by his wife. The year 1963 proved in many
ways an annus mirabilis. I met both "objectivists,"
Zukofsky and George Oppen. And those meetings
were preluded by two others—with Robert Duncan
and Robert Creeley.

Yet it was not to these previous meetings that I
owed my introduction to Zukofsky's poems: the
meetings confirmed what I was now ready for. What
remains difficult to explain in retrospect—in any
retrospect—is the way one's scattered awarenesses
suddenly fuse and focus. Perhaps it was further talk
with that indefatigable and indispensable negotiator
between cultures, Dr. Turnbull, whom I had last seen
in Gloucestershire and who now turned up in Albuquerque where I was teaching at the University of
New Mexico. At all events, in the autumn of 1962 I
began to realize once more the extent of my ignorance about the work of Zukofsky and about what
had been going on when in 1930, as Williams tells us
in his biography,

with Charles Reznikoff and George Oppen in an apartment
on Columbia Heights, Brooklyn, we together inaugurated,
first the Objectivist theory of the poem and then the Ob-

jectivist Press. . . . The Objectivist theory was this: we had had "Imagism" (Amygism, as Pound had called it), which ran quickly out. That, though it had been useful in ridding the field of verbiage, had no formal necessity in it. . . . It had dribbled off into so called "free verse" which, as we saw, was a misnomer. . . . Thus the poem had run down and become formally nonextant. . . . The poem being an object. . . . it must be the purpose of the poet to make of his words a new form. . . . This was what we wished to imply by Objectivism, an antidote, in a sense, to the bare image haphazardly prescribed in loose verse.

Present at that meeting on Columbia Heights (the apartment in question had been George and Mary Oppen's) was Louis Zukofsky, and it fell to him to outline in his essays a set of working principles. Since then he had gone on writing but was still largely unread.

Late in 1962 I tried interlibrary loan and early in 1963 the system disgorged a pristine copy of *Some Time*. This was the handsome edition put out by Jonathan Williams in 1956, and one thing a quick glance confirmed was that, though this was the seventh year of its existence, no one had ever cut the pages. This realization blinded me—quite literally as I was to discover in a few minutes—with sudden anger, and rushing into the kitchen for a sharp knife, I carved the pages apart in a crescendo of fury: such was the fate of poetry in a public library—once obtained, it was left unread. When calm returned and I sat down to lose myself in the book, I was surprised to discover that every time I turned the page two

blank pages appeared. Anger and surprise, combined,
had so reduced my faculties that it was quite some
minutes before I realized that what I had carved apart
was Jonathan Williams's beautiful intentions, and that
the immaculate candor of these backs of pages printed
on only one side had never been intended to be read.
Shame replaced surprise, then shame too gave way as
my eyes were invaded by the lovely and exact pleasure of

> Not the branches
> half in shadow
>
> But the length
> of each branch
>
> Half in shadow
>
> As if it had snowed
> on each upper half

—as visually precise as, over the page (or rather over
the page and two blanks), the following was aurally
meticulous:

> Hear, her
> Clear
> Mirror,
> Care
> His error.
> In her
> Care
> Is clear

—a weighing of tones to be reechoed, perhaps, in the

"Ears err for fear of spring" passage from Basil Bunting's *Briggflatts* ten years on.

In these two pieces, one had both sides of Zukofsky's gift, as stated (in reverse order) in *"A" 6:*

The melody! the rest is accessory:

My one voice. My other: is
An objective—rays of the object brought to a focus. . . .

I had the clue and so I read on, but it is difficult to disentangle the effect of that reading from the experience of another book which came unexpectedly and almost immediately after to hand. This was George Oppen's *The Materials*—his first for twenty-five years. Was this dual discovery what André Breton meant by objective chance? In actuality, it was a treble discovery, for out of the same, largely depressing pile of books that lay on my desk for review, emerged Reznikoff's *By the Waters of Manhattan*. I could begin now to reconstruct what had happened in those far-off days in Brooklyn and to see how it was still an active, though temporarily forgotten force in the America of the sixties. Zukofsky and Reznikoff had gone on publishing, but their books had been hard to come by. It was Oppen who was the real mystery—a mystery that has subsequently been explained—since all that one could find out about previous publication was that volume of 1934 ("Oppen's first book of poems," as it said on the cover of *The Materials*), which had earned the praise of Ezra Pound: "a sensibility . . . which has not been got out of any other

man's books." The existence of that first book—
instanced but unnamed on the cover—tantalized
more and more as I prepared to write the review. On
the track of Zukofsky, I had come upon Oppen,
whose work showed something of the same terse
lineation and exactness I had discovered just before in
Zukofsky's "Not the branches/half in shadow." On
an impulse I wrote to Oppen, who, in replying, offered me one of his three remaining *Discrete Series,*
that first book of poems, and said of the writing of
*The Materials* (his unaffected eloquence struck me as
one of the classic statements of modern poetry):

I was troubled while working to know that I had no sense
of an audience at all. Hardly a new complaint, of course.
One imagines himself addressing his peers, I suppose—
surely that might be the definition of 'seriousness'? I would
like, as you see, to convince myself that my pleasure in
your response is not plain vanity but the pleasure of being
heard, the pleasure of companionship, which seems more
honorable.

Those last two sentences so held my mind, I wanted
in some sense to appropriate them, as one does when
learning a passage by heart. They were so close to
being a poem, I could both appropriate them to my
own need and leave them in the hands of their author,
simply by arranging them as lines of verse, changing
only the pace yet leaving every word intact. This
poem ("To C. T.") was to appear ultimately in Oppen's third volume, *This in Which.* It drew the immediate response from him:

I find myself entranced by the poem with which you have presented me. I see myself—slightly the elder of the two of us—talking to myself—and smoking *my* pipe, which is a shock. I congratulate the three of us on the whole thing.

Another letter, in which he outlined for me the history of the objectivists—an account he much amplifies in an interview for *Contemporary Literature* (Spring, 1969), contains the following:

We were of different backgrounds; led and have led different lives. As you say, we don't much sound alike. But the common factor I think is well defined in Zuk's essay ["Sincerity and Objectification"]. And surely I envy still Williams' language, Williams' radiance; Rezi's lucidness, and frequently Zukofsky's line-sense.

My mind went back continually to a phrase in that first letter—"I was troubled to know I had no sense of an audience at all." If Oppen's sense of an audience had been an absence, what was Zukofsky's in the poems of *Some Time?* Occasionally it seemed to be almost wholly domestic—as witnessed by those valentines and the frequent family references. But, as I was to learn later, Zukofsky could count on an audience among the circle around *Black Mountain Review,* and its editor Robert Creeley was one of his most convinced readers. When Creeley returned from British Columbia to teach at the University of New Mexico in June 1963, I asked him, in a conversation we taped, what he felt had been Zukofsky's principal lesson for the younger poet. Creeley responded to that question in terms rather different from Oppen's

own stressing of the value of Zukofsky's critical sense
and the stimulus of his conversation, which were
what his letters mainly dwelt upon. For Creeley,
Zukofsky chiefly ratified in his poetry one side of the
teaching of Ezra Pound:

What Zukofsky has done [said Creeley] is to take distinc-
tions of both ear and intelligence to a fineness that is
difficult. . . . It's extremely difficult to follow him when
he's using all the resources that he has developed or inher-
ited regarding the particular nature of words as sound. . . .
If you read his translations of Catullus in which he is trying, in effect, to transpose or transliterate, or whatever the
word would be, the texture of Latin sound into American
language, it's an extraordinary *tour de force*. No, I find that
in this whole thing that Pound came into—the tone leading
of vowels, the question of measure, the question of the
total effect in terms of sound and sight of a given piece
of poetry—these aspects are tremendously handled by
Zukofsky as by no one else.

A couple of days after talking to Creeley, I set out
for Kiowa Ranch, on a mountainside beyond Taos. It
had been the gift of Mabel Dodge Luhan to D. H.
Lawrence and now belonged to the University of
New Mexico. In the period I was to spend there, from
June 22 to July 27, I had ample time and quiet to ab-
sorb the books Creeley had lent me—Zukofsky's
*Anew* and *"A" 1–12.* I copied by hand most of the
former and parts of the latter—mainly *"A" 7* and
*"A" 11,* which still seem to me Zukofsky's two most
impressive sections from that long poem. Kiowa
Ranch, the sea-wash sound in its pine trees, the

slightly inebriating sense of height, the long horizons, the slow withdrawals of the sunset to a band of deep orange above the far mesas—all these entered into my reading and copying. I found myself composing a poem to Zukofsky and enclosed in my first letter to him

> *To Louis Zukofsky*
>
> The morning
> spent in
>
> copying
> your poems
>
> from *Anew*
> because that
>
> was more
> than any
>
> publisher would
> do for one,
>
> was a
> delight: I
>
> sat high
> over Taos
>
> on a
> veranda
>
> Lawrence had
> made in
>
> exile here
> exile
>
> from those
> who knew

how to write
only the way they

had been
taught to:

I put aside
your book

not tired
from copying but

wishing for
the natural complement

to all the
air and openness

such art
implied:

I went
remembering that

solitude
in the world

of letters
which is yours

taking
a mountain trail

and thinking
is not

poetry
akin to walking

for one
may know

the way that

he is going

(though I did not)
without

his knowing
what he

will see there:
and who

following on
will find

what you
with more than

walker's care
have shown

was there
before his

unaccounting eyes?

In a letter of 1964, Louis was to suggest emending "(though I did not) / without / his knowing / what he" to "(though I / did not) / not knowing / what he," in order to "make it even lighter": "Give it a thought —or more than one—if you reprint in a volume—I may very likely be wrong." Then he added with characteristic elusiveness: "I just hope eels will never eat electrons or they might end up in my mad house." The reply to the poem suggested a meeting in New York on my way back in August. It also told me that he had been reading my work since 1957 ("and I find it valid. I can read it—which is to be moved—as Ez used to say. And for the rest Prospero had better shut

up about Miranda's accomplishments—just go ahead
and prosper." But he was to continue trying to improve Miranda's accomplishments. A later poem,
"Gull"—it emerged from seeing one over Brooklyn
harbor—which I dedicated to Louis and Celia, was
thoroughly relineated and compacted by him from its
first version, so that the poem as it now stands is as
much a work of collaboration as Oppen's "To C. T."
In fact, it so bears Louis's stamp, I have wondered
sometimes whether it ought not to ride one day in his
*Collected:*

> Flung
> far down,
> as the
> gull rises,
> the black
> smile of
> its shadow
> masking its
> underside
> takes
> the heart
> into the height
> to hover
> above the ocean's
> plain-of-mountains'
> moving quartz.

The letter which contained his revised version bore
the apologetic "about *Gull*—I probably shouldn't be
doing this, but what do *you* say?"—this ran vertically
down the right-hand side of the poem, then vertically

down the left: "(And I'm not so sure about align-
ment, but who's 'sure'?)." And beneath the poem:
"Anyway you moved me to do it fast." I thanked
him. He replied:

Thank me for? If you hadn't made it in potential, the stroke
[axshually, as the weather girl says, I did it very fast] of
genius (?) wouldn't have been actual. *No* time wasted, considering you agree—to be perfectly bumptious about it,
considering your gratitude makes me happy—and I never
take any credit from the prime mover. Don't tell anybody I
still do such things, however, or I'll be flooded who knows
with rafts of stuff from "pouncers."

I wasn't entirely sure what "pouncers" in inverted
commas implied. The idiom and rhythm of the letter
are very much those of Louis's speaking voice. The
bits you didn't understand in his rapid patter (he was
often extraordinarily comic) left you feeling you
ought to have, but there was no ling/ering for regret
or greater comprehension, because what he had gone
on to say now demanded your whole attention. You
couldn't afford to miss it. And just as you had to read
his letters at all angles for the tiny parentheses, you
often had to strain to hear his low-toned voice. His
whisper might be as funny as the minute postscript
down the back of an air letter: "C just bogged in income tax reports calls from downstairs to ask if we
can claim for being *blind*."

I was to hear that voice for the first time in August.
To begin with there had been doubts—doubts that
made me realize that Louis was already a frequently

sick man ("I'm ill so I can't move my head to left or right, but just to say it will have to improve by August 4, when you pass through"). There were to be several mentions of "the aches," not further defined, and three years later, in a letter saying that he had refused some teaching at Buffalo, I read the ominous words: "The emphysema won't bear the traffic." There had been more than doubts about seeing the Oppens that summer: it was a certainty they would be on Little Deer Isle, Maine. Then, suddenly, their plans were changed and they intended to be in Brooklyn. And, just as suddenly, our postal search for a New York apartment achieved success—that also was to be in Brooklyn. And though Brooklyn is a large place, as we soon knew, it was sufficiently the one place in which we would all coincide, the Zukofskys, the Oppens, and the Tomlinsons.

In *Kulchur* (Spring 1962) Jonathan Williams has an imaginary movie cast to play the modern poets— Edward Everett Horton as T. S. Eliot, Lon Chaney, Jr., as Robert Frost, Adolph Menjou as Edward Dahlberg, Cary Grant as James Laughlin. As Louis Zukofsky he casts Fred Astaire. There was an uncanny accuracy about this. Still showing signs of recent illness, Zukofsky had a curious dancing lightness in his build, movement, and talk. There was also a touch of elegance, given sartorial precision when ten days after our visit to 160 Columbia Heights, he turned up complete with bow tie at our apartment on Ocean Avenue. What did not fit Jonathan Williams's casting was the densely black, thick line of the eyebrows, the continuously relit cigarette, the nervous puckering of the forehead as the face flickered from anxiety to humor, the voluble, mercurial, ceaselessly inventive talk. That tenth story of Columbia Heights gave on to a view of the harbor. It was the same spot more or less that had seen the meeting of objectivists —not yet named—on that day in 1930. Through the window, behind Manhattan Bridge, loomed the span of Brooklyn Bridge. You could see it, but only just. The Statue of Liberty rose clear in the sultry August afternoon in the opposite direction. On the balcony the traffic noises floated up from below, often drowning out Zukofsky's soft voice.

We spoke of many things, including the funeral of William Carlos Williams the previous March ("The nicest funeral I ever went to," said Louis). But what most remains with me is the music of the occasion. By this I do not mean to reduce it to symbolist essence. "The greatest satisfactions of conversation are probably musical ones," as Ted Hughes has said. "A person who has no musical talent in ordinary conversation is a bore, no matter how interesting his remarks are. What we really want from each other are those comforting or stimulating exchanges of melodies." The music of meeting Zukofsky was exactly right, and one was encouraged to play one's few bars of accompaniment with a sense of satisfaction at having come in at the right place. His stream of talk was not exactly a monologue—he was too aware of one's presence for that—but it flowed and flashed and glowed in such a way that one hesitated to interrupt it.

Or, to change the metaphor, one suggested themes on which Zukofsky variated, very much for one's benefit and delight. There was a mutuality in this process which he evidently appreciated and remembered when two years later he wrote to me: "Hugh Kenner finally got to see us last week—just dropped in on a chance that I'd be at home, and we spent two afternoons together talking, the first talk of its kind I guess since you and I last talked. (The aches have been such we see almost nobody.)"

The talk at Columbia Heights gave place to his reading for us from his Catullus translations. As he did so, one realized that it was not only Pound that lay behind this venture, but principally the Joyce of *Finnegans Wake*. And Joyce came to mind in the quality of his vocal execution which compared with that light tenor rendering of the Anna Livia Plurabelle passage on gramophone record. The *Cats,* as he called them, came over as beautifully comic, though I could not help wondering whether, without the help of his expert vocalizing, and once extended from half a dozen to 116 plus fragmenta, these transliterations could hold the mind and not bring on a feeling of eels eating electrons. Here, he had pushed what he always called "the noise" of poetry about as far as it would go. Tune was his other favorite word:

> The lines of this new song are nothing
> But a tune making the nothing full

Do the tunes of the *Cats* survive in their author's voice? Did the Library of Congress perhaps tape some of them, when he recorded there? He would surely have wished them to be heard his way, the noise bringing to the surface a ghostly Roman gabble. He had written to Alfred Siegel in 1957 concerning Siegel's transliteration of the Chinese through Pound's Canto 97, "you mean the English *noises*[?], that would interest me."

The Zukofskys regaled us with trifle and cake, washed down with root beer, then walked with us through the twilight to find the bus stop. Louis was saying that his last communication from Ezra Pound was about a rabbi, then went on to define his attitude to the world of regular publishing from which he, Zukofsky, was as yet still excluded. "I don't care," was his frequent refrain, though I doubted that. There was a certain undertow of bitterness, though it never dominated the conversation. As we walked through the grimy yet reassuring streets of Brooklyn and finally took up our stand under the pole of the bus stop, it was gaiety that prevailed. We must have talked for half an hour before we realized that no buses intended to halt there and that the notice on top of the pole read "No Parking."

George Oppen is a man who came by knowledge with difficulty—which makes his Jewishness a very different thing from Zukofsky's. I recognized the latter's as soon as we had entered his apartment. It had the same flavor that had given point and aliment to my adolescence, when the refugees from Hitler's Germany arrived in the English Midlands. Here were people who had records of Bruckner and Brecht's

*Dreigroschenoper* at a time when both were unknown
to us. Among them I had heard Kant's categorical im-
perative explained as if it were a fact of daily life, had
listened to a description of Thomas Mann glimpsed
paring an apple "with surgical intentness," had discovered that Heine, Kafka, Rilke could still exist
among the coal dust and the fumes from pottery
chimneys. In this Jewishness one experienced a famil-
ial sense at once secretive and hospitable, subtly
tenser than one's own involvement in the painful day
to day of family bathos, where lack of money and
lack of imagination had produced a stale stoicism.
That experience of an eagerly tense intellectuality returned as one met the Zukofskys. Not so with the
Oppens.

To gain their apartment in Henry Street, one
passed the ground-floor window where a pleasant-
looking young man sat writing, as George later told
me, pornographic fiction. The scarred hallway and
stair led up to the top of the house and at the stairhead
stood a man with a lined and weathered face like a
Jewish sea captain—a man who, as it transpired,
owned a sailing boat but no car. This was George
Oppen. Like Zukofsky, he saw the humorous side of
things, but he listened more. His speech was less flu-
ent, more meditative; it was exact with a pondered exactness like his poetry.

We talked much of Mexico that evening—for we
had been there earlier the same year—and of the Oppens' phase of exile in Mexico City and his joinery
shop there. In his talk one warmed to a union of the
passionate and the deliberate: there was accuracy and

there was economy in this, and somehow, in one story he told us, he had managed to carry these to a point where they seemed like miracle or luck. Tired of the way Mexican drivers aimed their cars at you, George, crossing the Zócalo, had once refused to submit to this humiliation and, as the projectile approached, planted his fist square in the windshield: it was not the fist but the windshield that shattered. "A stupid thing to do," said George. The owner of the car got out, apparently for the showdown, but looking first at Oppen and then at the shivered glass, could find no way in which *machismo* could account for, admit, or take action against such folly, shrugged, reascended, and drove off. George has a genius for such inevitabilities. They need not always be the fruit of happy violence. In England, nine months after our meeting, the Oppens were at Ozleworth on an afternoon when the vicar called. Conversation turned on the New English Bible, and I expended a good deal of wasted wrath on our pastor's admiration for this moribund document. He explained that in order to make sure that its idiom was truly current the committee had consulted a bishop's secretary. George was far more of a marksman than I with my incoherent rage. As the vicar was about to leave, George said with a sort of courteous finality, "The next time you translate the Bible, call in a carpenter—and make sure he's a Jewish carpenter." Later, walking down the nave of Wells Cathedral, he gave vent to another unexpected apophthegm: "I guess I'm a Christian," he said, "but with all the heresies."

The apartment in Henry Street was very much a

presence in our conversation on that first encounter. As we sat eating, the evening moved into possession of the scene outside. High above Brooklyn, we watched the sun go down to the right of the Statue of Liberty, swiftly like a coin into a slot. Light shone from the statue's torch and from the windows of Manhattan—these of a strange greenish hue as if an effect taken up from the water in the summer dusk. Across the bay the Staten Island ferry stitched back and forth, a trail of lights above the milky turquoise it was travelling over. The television antennae on the near roofs of Brooklyn looked like ships' masts drawn up before the harbor below. This was a room and a view we were to revisit several times before the Oppens left for San Francisco in 1969, when Henry Street was threatened with demolition. The place seems a cell in a larger aggregate, from which memory picks out the building in a street close by where Whitman printed *Leaves of Grass,* now a Puerto Rican restaurant; the commemorative plaque on its wall (stolen, sold, and then recovered); the walk past red Edward Hopperish street facades; what *The Materials* calls "the absurd stone trimming of the building tops"; the site of the old Brooklyn ferry and behind its delapidated stakes the line of Brooklyn Bridge—Whitman superimposed on Hart Crane.

As the shapes of Manhattan hardened into black that evening, I began to realize that all was not well between Oppen and Zukofsky, and the impression deepened on subsequent meetings with them both. I think I may now speak of this, for George's poem with which I shall close makes no secret of the matter. When I reviewed Reznikoff's and Oppen's books I had wondered why there was no Zukofsky in the series, a joint publication of New Directions (James Laughlin) and *San Francisco Review* (June Oppen Degnan, George's half sister). His exclusion there clearly rankled with Louis. Even before I had met him, I realized the situation was an uneasy one, for, after sending my review to Oppen, I had received the following reply:

I enjoyed very much reading your review. . . . I will have a copy made for New Directions-SF Review for the mention of Zuk. . . . The first year's poetry schedule consists of Oppen, Reznikoff and William Bronk, in which my advice is obvious enough. My recommendation of course included Zuk, but the suggestion—as you see—has not been acted on. It is by now too awkward for me to discuss the matter with Zuk at all, but it is my impression that they would be more likely to do a Selected than a Collected poems, if only for budgetary reasons. I can't really urge Louis to submit a ms. since I have no assurance at all that they would accept it. But you might urge him to try it if you think it worth the risk—to him—of a rejection. If they had a ms. under consideration I could re-open the discussion.

When I arrived in New York, I had some illusory hopes that I might perhaps be able to negotiate on Louis's behalf. As I stayed on, this hope extended to the possibility of somehow reconciling the estranged friends. But the longer I stayed the more I realized that neither project could be easily accomplished. In the first place, not only his self-respect but also Louis's belief that all his life he had been writing *one* poem (and he was very decided about this) stood in the way of my ever persuading him to submit a selected, and secondly, his feelings toward George had curdled to such an extent that any reconciliation must lie far in the future if it were feasible at all. From hints and suggestions, I gathered that he imagined George had simply failed to act for him, which was not the case. Yet one could not simply *state* this to Louis. He did not live in the atmosphere of simple statement and his aggravated nerves pushed him into more suspicion than was good for him. He was a gentle man, yet his own character and long neglect had created a thorny hedge of self-defense and of self-injury. Years of teaching what he called "my plumbers" at the Brooklyn Polytechnic Institute cannot have helped: "My own mess of school etc is proverbial," he wrote, complaining of chalk fights and "kids of seventeen who cannot sit on their asses." "All I need is to be away from that 'job' I guess—the eellectermonickers, curs, curse." Perhaps he even resented the fact that George was at last free from the job grind. It is hard to be certain. At all events, he made it clear that no interference, however delicate, could help repair the situation. I unwillingly resigned myself to this fact.

On returning home, I set about sharing my new-found knowledge of things American with my fellow countrymen, or as many of them as read the little magazines. For *the Review*, January 1964, I edited a

Black Mountain poetry number in which Louis figured as one of the founding fathers. Ian Hamilton, the regular editor, added his own characteristic postscript: "The editorial motive of *the Review* in this project has been a documentary rather than, necessarily, a critical one. We believe that the movement ought at least to be known about." So much for English caution, incapable of surrendering itself to surprise. The following December appeared the Louis Zukofsky issue of *Agenda*. All this time I kept up a regular correspondence with Louis and an exchange of books. He was an excellent critic and immediately perceptive about where another poet's strengths lay. His method of instruction by letter consisted of copying out the individual phrases which had struck him as centrally strong. I mentioned one poem of mine which he had not touched on and he replied, "I was trying to point at *that* in your work which might now be more useful to you as 'craft,' when you've extended it *past* your forefathers." On my *Peopled Landscape* he wrote: "As for prosody a little nearer Hardy in impulse of song rather than for all I revere his integrity the thought metres of Crabbe—and so on, the old guy's talking too much." He emphasized that it was "the 'pure' of the craft" he was interested in revealing to one, and on the poem to which I had drawn his attention: " 'Craft' as 'invention' etc. In itself the poem is nothing to be neglected and in a work like my Test of Poetry would do very well alongside of Crabbe and Marvell . . . ." He could respond unexpectedly to poems whose premises were very un-

Zukofskyan, as when he pointed to one of mine called "The Impalpabilities" and added "[would be your best defence against *Bottom*]." His square brackets managed to be at once intimately playful and also defensive of another's interests, a typical example of the atunement of his epistolary style and also of his conversation (he was a man who could *speak* square brackets) to the needs of a friend. Of friends' needs he was always studious. His caring ranged from minute, attentive sympathy (on hearing my father was ill, he inquired about him for many letters after) to a sense of troubles taken on his own behalf. It could be simply a question of a meal. Or it could be a friend's luck that brightened his feelings, as when Bunting finally achieved publication with Fulcrum Press: "I hope Basil gets the garter or sumpin—anything to save him from the dogged silence he's lived. It makes him happy—at any rate he writes cheerfully—to have some attention. *Loquitur* is a beautiful book, and *Briggflatts* is a delayed extension of it." And there were friends missed. Of Williams he spoke with great affection, for Williams, while not quite getting what Louis was at, had always written of him with generosity. One document of their literary relations I discovered while editing the *Agenda* issue—this was a signed statement of Williams's of June 29, 1948, which ran: "I hereby grant formal permission to Louis Zukofsky to use whatever he wishes to use of my published literary works as quotations in his writings."

In the winter of 1964 Louis began to talk of retirement. They were to move to two-and-a-half rooms:

"Kitchen, living room with an L for sleeping. We've been living to pay the rent and income tax. The idea is to get down—to something like a bare table top—and maybe something of the feeling of 30 years ago where we wandered the streets of the same neighborhood, rather young, will come back to us." By August I heard: "We're delighted to be in Manhattan again after 25 years. . . . the streets have all the interest of a foreign city to provincials." The same letter contained the news of acceptance by Norton of his poems ("First publication of poetry since they did Rilke in 1938 . . .") and of a further bonus that Reznikoff had just telephoned to read out a long and positive review of *Bottom* in the *TLS*—"very careful and painstaking. . . . So your country gets there ahead of mine." I hesitated to confess (those were the days of anonymity) that I had written it.

Though Louis continued to feel the loneliness of his position, a period of respite seemed to be ensuing for him. Not that all was plain sailing now. The advance from Norton hadn't, as he wrote, "covered half the medico's bill." Yet there was freedom from the plumbers and there was a December visit to Yaddo in 1965 to finish the *Cats:* "Silence helps—only a handful of reticent respectful guests—so far we can stand the cold. Pines, trails, waterfalls, high views from the foothills of the Adirondacks, and altogether too many good books around with no time to read if I'm to get through with that Guy (Gai)."

In the meantime I had been planning an anthology. If I could not help to reconcile George and Louis, at any rate I could surely get them together inside the covers of one book. And this book would show English readers an area of American poetry with which they were not as yet familiar. The title, *Seven Significant Poets,* embraced the objectivists (Oppen, Zukofsky, Reznikoff, and Carl Rakosi), Lorine Niedecker (characterized in *"A" 12* as "a rich sitter"), James Laughlin, and William Bronk.

I was in New York in the spring of 1966 and so able to speak with Louis about this idea. Our meeting took place at 77 Seventh Avenue. "You must come to the biggest Vermeer you've ever seen and you'll find us," he said over the telephone. The Vermeer proved to be an enormous blowup of one of his paintings used as a mural decoration for the downstairs vestibule of the apartment building. It still looked solidly composed but uncomfortably stretched. The apartment was overheated, at least for English susceptibilities, and Louis seemed ill, though still full of inventive talk. The meeting was attended by a lingering uneasiness. We were staying with the Oppens, a fact not easy to declare, and when the Zukofskys invited us to remain to dinner the awkwardness arose of phoning our hosts from the one room that we would not be back for an evening meal. This I accomplished with absurd secretiveness and put down the phone, having mentioned no names. "So you're staying with the Oppens," said Louis. Yet the awkwardness passed and a pleasant meal followed. Louis seemed interested by the idea of the anthology, though he didn't care for the work of Bronk—"All that Stevensian bothering.

You either think with things as they exist, or you give up." "Is Oppen in it?" called Celia from the kitchen. Louis seemed to accept that fact as inevitable also. I was not so sure that Celia did. But the way ahead looked clear and there was even a sort of geniality in Louis's contemplation of the prospect.

Back in England I put several months' work into the book and Fulcrum expressed their wish to publish it. When they approached Louis for permission to reprint, there came back a firm no in reply. It wasn't entirely unexpected, but one had hoped that, if reconciliations were not possible in daily life, perhaps literary works could still lie down amicably side by side. I never discussed the matter further with Louis, though obviously, without his presence in the book, it must remain a total impossibility. I'd simply spent a great deal of time to little effective end. We continued to correspond with perfect cordiality though we never met again. I should have foreseen the difficulties in the light of George's letter three years before concerning Louis's diatribes against him to innocent visitors:

But perhaps I had better say that Louis really has no grievance against me, nor has the world, or no greater grievance than it has against anyone in these times of population explosion. And Louis no greater grievance against me than against anyone who "gets printed." Awkward for me, tho. And overwhelmingly ironic to discuss my position as "a success". . . . I doubt that I'll produce another book within quite a few years. Maybe that'll heal things.

That was after *The Materials*. Other books followed and finally a collected. But so did books by

Louis, including the two volumes of *All*. Clearly he
was right to have resisted a selection. He got what he
wanted, but what a time it took. And time didn't, in
George's words, "heal things." When George gave
me his *Collected Poems* in San Francisco in 1976 I
found in it, toward the close, a poem I had not read
before. I thought perhaps I had missed it in his previous collection, *Seascape: Needle's Eye,* but, no, it is not
there. The title is "The Lighthouses" and the subtitle
"for LZ in time of the breaking of nations":

> *if you want to say no say*
> *no if you want to say yes say yes* in loyalty
>
> to all fathers or joy
> of escape
>
> from all my fathers. . . .

and the poem modulates into George's seaboard
world where lighthouses flash and the coastal waters
are rock-pierced. He recognizes the kinship with
Zukofsky—for Zukofsky was in a sense one of his
fathers too, a brilliant exemplar and talker in the early
days of objectivism. He recognizes also the racial kinship as a motif returns, previously used in the poem
"Semite":

> my
> heritage *neither Roman*
> *nor barbarian*. . . .

I do not know whether Louis ever read the piece or
whether, had he done so, he would have recognized
George's continuing plea for clarity in relationship.

"The Lighthouses" is a final document in a long and saddening history of misunderstanding, a misunderstanding which a common experience of a time, place, and race might have outweighed but did not. It reminded me of the fact that from both their windows in Brooklyn they had shared the view of the same "lighthouse"—the beam from the statue shining back in the dusk towards the windows of Manhattan.

# 3
# A Late Greeting: O'Keeffe

The envelope was addressed in a strong hand which might have been masculine. The dictionary defines calligraphy as elegant penmanship. This was certainly calligraphy, but it was forceful rather than elegant, and the diagonal "Do Not Bend," with its firmly scalloped underlining like an ideogram for "choppy sea," proclaimed authority. No one had bent the contents of the envelope despite its ample size. The card within carried the message "A late greeting / I hope it reaches you" and the monogram "G. O'K." Georgia O'Keeffe's Christmas card—or was it a New Year greeting?—had been mailed on January 20, 1964, and arrived in England in time for spring, having been readdressed from Albuquerque, where we were no longer residents. The illustration consisted of one of her early watercolors, *Starlight Night* of 1917, scarcely a couple of years after Alfred Stieglitz's discovery of her with his celebrated remark, "Finally a woman on paper." It was the sort of starlight night you might find six thousand feet above sea level in the crystalline air of Abiquiu, New Mexico, from where the card had been mailed.

This was the second postal communication that I had received from Miss O'Keeffe—always "Miss O'Keeffe," never "Mrs. Stieglitz" ("Why should I take on someone else's famous name?"). The first— before we had met—had been a Western Union telegram: "Please come Sunday at eleven for lunch." That unexpected summons to the high village forty miles north of Santa Fe in January 1963 marked a stage on a journey that had begun seventeen years before—also in January—when Donald Reid had sent me (it was my nineteenth birthday) *An Illustrated Handbook of Art History*. In a postwar England not rich in exotic books and in Blackpool, not conspicuous for its bookshops, the unaccountable presence of the compilation by Frank J. Roos, Jr., had caught his eye. What caught mine, on receiving it, was the unknown quantity, American art. Thus, when long afterward I came to read Lowell's poem "For the Union Dead," Augustus Saint-Gaudens's Shaw Memorial, which is in question there, was no stranger to me, though I had never seen it in the flesh, or more exactly, in the bronze.

Not that the Saint-Gaudens had ever made for me a forceful image. What held the eye was the outline of American painting—Homer, Ryder, Eakins, then (approaching the present) Marin, three Demuths, and a single O'Keeffe, *The Mountain*. This last, indifferently reproduced like all the plates, two by three inches and in monochrome, entered one's meditations. In it, all the sinews of the mountain stood revealed. It seemed to have heaved upward and fallen sideways like a sleeper who has just turned over. And yet it was not in any way personified. The colors, reduced uniformly to grey, except for some darker tree shapes and was it the sky above or a larger mountain containing this smaller one?—the colors could have been those of ice or fire. What the printing could not eliminate was the firm articulation of the musculature, the rock-thrust, the held declivities, the sense of an even light bringing the whole to bear. This was my first glimpse of the landscape of New Mexico, although I had no way of identifying the place or the painter. Indeed, *The Mountain* was flanked by Eugene Speicher's *Portrait of a Girl,* which memory misread as *Portrait of an Irish Girl,* so that for years I carried with me this quite erroneous picture of O'Keeffe. More profitably, I came to associate *The Mountain* with Marianne Moore's poem "An Octopus," where an entire mountain mass is "gone over," with its octopus of ice on top " 'Creeping slowly as with meditated stealth, / its arms seeming to approach from all directions.' " So evidently it was ice color the grey reproduction had suggested. Wrong again, but the wrongness scarcely injured the picture of the landscape it essentialized although both were the color of fire. The form rode in the mind unimpaired until it was to blaze back at me from the outside at a first sight of the Sangre de Cristo Mountains abrupt above the New Mexican desert.

"Please come Sunday at eleven for lunch." It seemed a generous invitation. Whoever heard of going to lunch until twelve-thirty? I had not expected

such a wide margin for talk. To begin with, I had
expected very little. For whenever I had raised the
question of trying to see O'Keeffe, people had shaken
their heads. "You will find it difficult to get in. She
sees very few except her friends." Yet the desire per-
sisted. Having carried that image in one's head for the
better part of twenty years, having come through it to
an aspect of modern painting one's countrymen had
never inspected, one had perhaps earned a meeting. It
was my friend, the poet Winfield Townley Scott,
who brought it about. I had been admiring a book of
photographs of ghost towns in his house at Santa Fe.
The photographer was Todd Webb—"a close friend
of O'Keeffe's," as Win added. I reiterated my half-
forlorn hope. "I'll call him for you and see what he
suggests." The next thing I knew, a week later, was
that I had in my hand a telegram from the great lady.

That winter had been relatively mild. There had
been snow and sleet on Christmas Eve, but one had
driven with comparative ease, though through cling-
ing mud, to mass at the pueblo church of San Felipe.
After the service, there had been dancing, the dancers
entering at the huge west door preceded by the soft-
timbred music of their ankle bells, their coyote yelps
sharp on the snowy air. One was aware of the vast
space behind them, and then the explosion of a Kiowa
war dance, all energy and feathers, blotted it back into
the cold night as six drummers and chorus accompanied the dancers into the resonating church.
Christmas Day saw deep, brilliant snow. Then the
weather turned kind once more. A week before the

visit to Abiquiu I sat in warm sun watching the deer and antelope dances on the plaza of Cochiti pueblo. It seemed like summer and the whole ceremony took on a mesmerically summery glow to the beat of a single drum. The light sought out the white tunics and the red headbands of the line of male dancers in their doeskin boots. The two Deer Mothers, one at either end of the line, flared in red blouses, the left shoulder bare, turquoise round their necks, head-feathers, black kirtles, white puttees. Under the full sun of morning, the two women advanced from the line of dancing men to be met by two deer—male dancers whose forelegs were completed by their bending over on sticks. They moved in fascinated dependence on the Deer Mothers, behind them two bright-blanketed priests. The Deer Mothers drew them without noticing them, with solemn, lowered eyes and an impersonal, sexless dignity. In their hands they carried bunches of feathers and the deer imitated their circular gestures with identical motions of the neck. The weather was part of the ceremony—a slow hypnosis of pulsating sunlight. But it wouldn't last.

The day before I set out for Abiquiu followed a night below zero in the Albuquerque valley. Someone going home drunk had entangled himself in barbed wire and frozen to death. The next night would be even colder, we were told, and it was—down to thirty below, just north of Santa Fe; and at Albuquerque, the breathtaking rareness of snow air and snow light in a snowbound city.

The car was immoveable. Even had it been other-

wise, who could say what the weather would be like
at Abiquiu? Thirty below. But that was at Tesuque.
Also north of Santa Fe. But Abiquiu lay further to the
west. One would be late at all events. The generosity
of "come at eleven" put one in the wrong from the
start. But what was the use of going back and forth
over the situation? The weather was immoveable,
too. The air seemed to encase one in a suit of ice.
There was not even a whisper from the car battery.
Other cars stood on their driveways like stranded
boats. The streets were empty.

But one had failed to take into account the desert
sun. Once it was above the mountains, the snow
began to melt until it lay only in the shadows, a white
geometry at the edges of buildings reproducing ga-
bles and rooflines on the shining black streets. The
immoveable car was dragged, pushed, coaxed into
motion, coughed a little, jerked, came unjammed,
faded dangerously, was forced back into life by a diligent foot. It was impossible to get there by eleven, if
one could get there at all. But the car was moving, the
snow was sliding off the roofs, the way through town
was clear, and out into the desert the paved highway
shone and steamed as the sun drew off its snow. The
oranges and reds of the desert were seeping back now
through the retreating white. Water sang and flashed
through the *arroyos* under the road. The sun was feeling once more for the shapes of the immense arid
landscape in which the wet from the snowfall had
flushed up the dusty colors like water thrown over a
mosaic floor. Among the ghostly greys of the winter

cottonwood trees, behind the tin-roofed adobes, along the banks of the snow-filled Rio Chama, everything rekindled, glittered, sending up mica showers, crossing blades of light. Light that had been snow. Snow that underscored the reefs of orange rock. It was the dance of fire and ice. The tall blue of the sky was reestablished, though even the sun could not entirely blunt the sharpened air.

Abiquiu, or Santo Tomás Apostel de Abiquiu, lies twenty miles from the town of Española. Before Highway 84 was paved, it must have seemed fifty. Within living memory the journey there and back took at least three days, and coming to each *arroyo,* a wagon would need to be unloaded and reloaded on the further bank. The story is told by Gilberto Benito Cordova* of the horse-drawn wagon stuck and abandoned in El Arroyo de Oso. Two cousins, inhabitants of Abiquiu, approaching the spot from opposite directions, began an extended argument about the wagon's real color, finally threatening each other with physical violence. The son of the cousin who had approached from the Abiquiu side tried the experiment, while the argument was at its height, of tickling one of the horses under its tail with his stick, the result being that the team suddenly started forward and freed the cart, revealing that each side of it was painted a different color.

Abiquiu still seems set apart. It consists of the crumbling remains of an eighteenth-century settle-

*\*Abiquiu and Don Cacahuate: A Folk History of a New Mexican Village* (Cerrillos, New Mexico: San Marcos Press, 1973).

ment of Genízaros, that is, Hispanicized Indians of
mixed tribal origins. The word is an etymological relation of the Turkish *janissaries*—Christians turned
into Islamic soldiers by the Turks. The car, slithering
into the muddy ruts of the village street, found its
way by a kind of instinct to a long, low wall behind
which sheltered a long, low house, to a gateway
adorned by an immense deer skull complete with
branching antlers. It brought to mind O'Keeffe's
painting, *From the Faraway Nearby,* where the sky is
filled with a horned, floating skull, behind it the
empty blue, and bare desert hills beneath. Evidently
one had come to the right place. Bone by adobe.
When I admired the trophy at the gate later that afternoon, she replied, "I swapped a hi-fi set for it."

I expected a tall woman. She was a vigorous
seventy-six, rather small of stature, with a mild but
incisive voice, the incisiveness toning the mildness of
its sound with a strength that could take itself for
granted. She talked readily, easily. She smiled frequently with reconnaissant eyes, so that the lined face
of the photographs, with its thin, fine eyelids, possessed an animation that photography in freezing
banishes. One saw why Stieglitz had taken his five
hundred pictures of her, realizing the practicable part
of that dream of his of a photographic portrait that
ideally should start with birth, follow out a life to
death, and then begin once more with the child of the
subject. I was late and I expected her to be displeased,
but that day all her guests had arrived late—Todd
Webb with his wife, and a granddaughter of Mabel
Dodge Luhan with her husband. We had been talking

of the great cold when O'Keeffe said to me in the same voice with which she spoke of the weather, "You got in on false pretenses. I am not friendly. I thought you were a friend of Todd Webb's." I had just met Todd Webb for the first time. The eyes seemed to acknowledge that she was half-joking. I wasn't sure. In retrospect, she seems merely to have been stating the truth of the matter. But neither was she *un*friendly now that I'd "got in."

The house was a rambling adobe. The room in which we sat talking, and the adjoining room in which we ate, were painted a stark white. Black vases from San Ildefonso pueblo contained grey twigs, flowerless. She, also, wore black, a masculine-looking trouser suit, and later, when we went outside, a thick black leather coat. On tables and ledges, animal bones of various sizes, stones very smooth and rounded. Dark furniture against white walls, an adobe-colored mud floor. Under low vigas two Chinese statues, two African masks, no O'Keeffes, no Stieglitz. There was a warren of smaller rooms. They had formerly been used as pigpens, being abandoned as the roofs fell in and then locked. She had bought the derelict house from the church, renovating the rooms one by one and building in each a differently sized fireplace to burn the aromatic *piñon* wood. The rooms had been plastered by local women. "They do the work best," she said; "They did the whole house. Every inch of its surface has been touched by a woman's hand. Now I have to think about the outside. Four years of rainy weather, and the adobe is melting away."

We ate well. Beef, salad, water-grown tomatoes,

pickled onions and curry, prepared by Amelia, her
helper; ice cream which she had made herself and
apologized for; mangoes which she had never served
previously, red wine, coffee. Assisting in carrying out
the dishes, one caught sight through the kitchen window of the enfiladed mesas commanding their
orange, juniper-stippled spaces with, in the foreground, on the kitchen table, a giant, black grinding-
stone, a *matata,* that had come from Amelia's grand-
mother.

Conversation had been easy and unforced at table,
but it had been general, and some of it impenetrably
local, so that I had the feeling that I had not really
been speaking to *her,* that perhaps this was the wages
of false pretenses. One item of local talk lodged in my
ear. It concerned the Indian husband of Mabel Luhan
who, as he lay on his deathbed, kept reiterating, "I
want to go to the rodeo at Cimarrón. Why don't
somebody take me there?" As the others drifted back
to the armchairs, O'Keeffe unexpectedly drew me
aside and over to the further end of the dining table:
"And now let's talk. And let me say first of all how
much I admire your green English tweed. What a
marvellous material."

We began by talking of the cubists. She had known
them early and admired Braque. Was that because of
the 1913 Armory Show? No. She had known them
before. She had seen them at Mr. Stieglitz's gallery
(she invariably referred to him as "Mr. Stieglitz") in
an elegant but plain brownstone house—Picasso and
Braque drawings, and other things one would wish to

see when young, including African things. "I had no great passions," she continued; "I went my own way. I didn't even intend to 'live' by painting because there's the danger that you'll try to copy the style of someone else and 'work' it." No, she didn't care for Constable, but loved Turner; hadn't, in fact, known many English people except for Gerald Heard. Thought England would be too green for her, like Virginia, where she had lived for a time. She had toured France—Chartres, Vézelay, Autun; Chartres with its big windows "like being under trees." "I think the architecture is the greatest achievement of the Church—finer than the frescoes, finer than Ravenna." I wanted to ask about Sheeler and Demuth but she spoke more of the city, of New York, in the twenties. "It was the end of brownstone Park Avenue (where you walked when you had a cold). As the skyscrapers took over, high and separate, they made you feel they'd fall on you." We talked a good deal of Abiquiu. "It's like living in a novel. Why, there's a mother here who won't let her child have a hearing aid because she's afraid it'll make his hearing worse." Most of all she spoke of Joe, the Spanish boy, now twenty, she'd been "bringing on." "I've had him get his teeth fixed and scraped. I give him brewer's yeast and molasses and it's improved his complexion and made him stand straight. And, after brewer's yeast, he works better. He's great with cars. He bought an old school bus for twenty dollars when he was eighteen—learned to fix and unfix it, and now he's an expert. I signed for him when he made a down pay-

ment on a truck. His uncle and grandfather would
have paid off the installments if Joe couldn't, but they
wouldn't *sign* anything."

Joe was to be in demand that afternoon. The other
two guests had departed, and Todd Webb's car
wouldn't start. So O'Keeffe asked me to drive her to
Joe's place, an adobe house beyond the village, in
search of the mechanic. "I go with him," she said,
"into the mountains to find watercress. I always find
the best, but I'm hoping to teach *him* to find it to save
myself." The afternoon was advancing and deep blue
shadows were gathering under the mesas and in the
fractures of the rocks, bringing everything to a pitch
of vivid abstraction in the sinking light. "The clarity,
that's what I love about this place," she said, as we
took in the lengthening, sharp shadows. "A pity," she
went on; "there's no time for you to see my ghost
ranch. It's sixteen miles up-country. You'd like the
landscape there." I asked her if it was there she first
began painting cattle bones. Her reply was, "You
know why I began painting cattle bones? I used to
come here summers, and the question was what to
take back to New York which would recall New
Mexico. I would have taken flowers, but at the height
of summer flowers were scarce. So I took bones and
painted them."

I had noticed that at least once she had painted
bones and flowers together in *Summer Days* of 1936.
Earlier still, in *Blue and Green Music* of 1919, a much
more abstract picture, there was a similar confronta-
tion of growth with death. This picture was fresh in
my mind, since I had been examining a slide of it on

the previous evening. Out of a concourse of rigid embattled triangles, there emerges in mid-canvas a billowing as if wind-torn area of whitish flame. It resembles, in its involved flickerings and flarings, the unravelling petals of a flower or the skins of an onion bulb. And there, crowning this spectral conflagration, one makes out the pun of a skull shape, squashed sideways, Holbein-wise, like the anamorphosis at the foot of his picture *The Ambassadors.* The whole is immaculately painted, a kind of mask of white death invading the formalized humanism of the cubists. I asked her in the car about this invasion. "No, I've never seen a skull there," she replied quietly as though pondering the matter, as though there *might* be a skull there, but unwilling to commit herself to one: "I didn't *know* there was a skull there."

Joe was not in. Joe's brother was, and would send Joe over when he reappeared. We drove back. "When Joe goes into the army," she said with decision, "I aim to try and bring on his brother."

It was getting late and cold and I had to start. First she insisted on showing the rest of the house with its whitewashed adobe fireplaces and Navajo rugs. Then she said in a tone that sounded like Miss Moore's, "I'll offer you tea before going, but I refuse to offer you alcohol." Almost her last remark was, "When you return to New Mexico, you must come in." Come in? It was an unexpected turn of phrase. "I am not friendly," I recalled, but friendly she *had* been, and "come in" suggested a full absolution from my false pretenses, the cordial opposite of "get in."

Whenever New Mexico reenters the mind, it

comes in images that are hers and images that are not
hers. One which is hers and which I can see clearly
with shut eyes is *Red Hills and Bones* of 1941, with its
dry vistas, the hill humps with their deep, parched
wrinkles full of shadow. Here, a vision that in *Blue
and Green Music* flickers with the underpresence of the
skull, grows calm, and the discarded fragments of an
animal's skeleton that lie across the foreground of the
picture do so in repose, in stillness and light, from the
exquisitely segmented spine of the foreground skeleton, through the ghosts of the autumnal chamiso
bushes behind to the barrenness of hill and rock mesa.
What is missing from the hills and what I saw against
the sky on the long drive back that night, rising from
the heaped-up boulders, is a Penitente cross. That
image also belongs to her, or to one aspect of her
work. For, the first summer she was able to pass entirely in New Mexico, that of 1929, saw the painting
of *Black Cross, New Mexico,* where the shape of a huge
Penitente cross dominates the recession of treeless,
rounded hills, the red and yellow bars of the sunset
imprisoned between its arms and the horizon of purple land. This black cross, held together by four massive nails, and the blood-colored sunset beneath it,
evoke the ascetic and tragic spirit of Los Hermanos de
la Luz, offshoot of the Third Order of St. Francis—
the New Mexico of the Penitente chapels, the *moradas*
where Death armed with bow and arrow sits waiting
in its wooden cart. In another picture, *Cross by the
Sea, Canada* of 1932, the cross is identical with those
one finds in any of the small Spanish *camposantos* of

New Mexico; the fence around it resembles precisely the fence of carved wooden pickets, *cuña* or *cerquita,* which surrounds a grave. The image that is not hers is the image of the Indian dance—behind her crosses rises the *morada,* not the church of San Felipe with its explosion of drums and feathers, or the dancing plaza where the drumbeat intercedes between heartbeat and sunbeat and unites them. One critic speaks of *Red Hills and the Sun* of 1927 as "nature imbued with a pantheistic, transcendent life of its own." The formula seems an improbable one for O'Keeffe, though it is not a new one, something like it already appearing in the review in *Camera Work* which greeted her first exhibition at Stieglitz's "291" gallery in 1917. If pantheism means anything, it is unitive like the communion of bloodbeat and drumbeat. O'Keeffe's is a separating vision giving her space in which to contemplate the thing before her. The magnified flower paintings and the abstracted interiors of *Jack-in-the-pulpit* in its several versions, though they are symbols for processes that involve and transcend the self, lack the oceanic engulfment of Jackson Pollock's early Indian-inspired totemic pictures and his later kinship with the Navajo sand painters pouring their images. They remain oddly literal in their strangeness and isolation, as irreducible as the black rock that fills three quarters of the canvas of *Black Rock with Blue* of 1970—like one of Magritte's magnified apples, though there is nothing here to indicate its actual scale or whether, indeed, it is magnified. The blue it bulks against is that which long ago she saw in all its inten-

sity through the holes in held-up pelvis bones, and of
which she wrote during the war ". . . that Blue that
will always be there as it is now after all man's de-
struction is finished."

She discovered herself during one war and has long
survived a second. She was born in the same year as
Miss Moore, 1887, a year before Eliot, two after
Pound, four after Williams. At ninety-one, she is the
last survivor of the great generation. All of these
poets had read their Fenollosa. And she, along with
Pound, owed much of the direction of her career to
his having written. Two statements:

This man had one dominating idea: to fill space in a beautiful way.

We find that all art is harmonious spacing under special
technical conditions that vary.

The first is O'Keeffe speaking of Arthur Wesley
Dow, whose book *Composition* and whose teaching
methods introduced the ideas of Fenollosa into American art schools. The second quotation is from Fenollosa's *Epochs of Chinese and Japanese Art,* and it sum-
marizes what he had been saying in the face of a
prevailing academicism ever since he had returned
from Japan in 1892 to become, first, curator of the
Boston Museum of Fine Arts, and then a popular lec-
turer. O'Keeffe gave up painting in 1912, but in the
summer of that year returned to it under the influence
of Alon Bement, a follower of Dow's. In 1914–15
she went, persuaded by Bement, to study with Dow
in New York, and again in the spring of 1916. Simul-

taneously, she was discovering the Southwest, teaching near Amarillo in Texas. It was at this moment that the spaces of Fenollosa and the spaces of the desert, of East and West, met in a ground for new harmonies, new dissonances. The stone garden of Ryōanji, the red cliffs of Tomieka Tessai, Hiroshige's red strip of sunset, waited to be rediscovered in America, in Abiquiu. As China's sacred mountain Taishan redeclared its form to an American mind from the mountains beyond the detention camp at Pisa.

"When you return to New Mexico, you must come in." I have returned to New Mexico twice since then, but I have not "come in." The first time was four years later and the visit was rushed, the second was thirteen and I imagined she would scarcely remember. Perhaps I should have risked it. She hadn't known many Englishmen, and she still recalled Gerald Heard in 1963. Perhaps there is still time. I have written these pages as, in some sense, a late greeting.

# 4
# *Dove Sta Memoria: In Italy*

Dove sta memoria

> till the stone eyes look again seaward
>> some minds take pleasure in counterpoint

—more talismanic fragments, to set beside "Pine-scent in snow-clearness." The book that contains them, *The Pisan Cantos,* I packed in my luggage on our first trip to Italy, 1951. The train passed through Pisa in an autumnal downpour. I looked out for the tower and caught not only that, but what the poem had prepared one for, standing apart from the mass of the cathedral: "a patch of the battistero all of a white-ness." The gloom scarcely muffled that whiteness and there was light enough to define the ribs of sharp, projecting stones that punctuate the conical dome and give it the spiky appearance of a sea urchin.

That—*dove sta memoria*—lies the better part of thirty years away. For the past twenty I have experienced, practically daily, another sight which draws the threads together and sets counterpoint into motion—that line of houses, Wortley Terrace, where, when it had not yet spilled beyond itself, Wotton-

under-Edge used to end. Sophie Brzeska, Henri
Gaudier's companion, lived there after his death and
before her removal to the Gloucester asylum. I had
passed the house for ten years before I saw at Brunnenberg Gaudier's head of Pound, as whitely commanding as that glimpse of Pisa, its stone eyes looking toward the mountains of the Upper Adige from
the garden of his daughter's castle.

Pleasure in counterpoint? Pleasure or pain or both.
The young Gaudier—but Gaudier was never not the
young Gaudier: the Gaudier who had not yet touched
marble used to climb the steps into Bristol Museum
to sketch the stuffed animals. I work on the other side
of the street and the reminder is always there.

The memory of that death is folded now in the
memory of another, a later one. In 1974, going down
from the exhibition, Vorticism and Its Allies, to the
ground floor of the Hayward Gallery where the photographs of Diane Arbus were to be seen, I met
Robert Lowell circulating this latter show in the opposite direction. We strolled out together and took
tea beside the Thames.

"You can see why she went mad," he said, refer-
ring to those pictures where nothing is ever quite
right even in the most ordinary scenes, and where
freakishness puts on such a daily face you could imagine it was the only possibility.

"What did you make of the vorticists?" I asked.

"Oh, pretty inhuman stuff."

I swallowed down argument, thinking of those
early abstracts of Wyndham Lewis, 1912 and 1913,

where passion so declares itself, free of all effusive-
ness, it cannot but get itself mistaken for coldness.

"What about Gaudier?"

"Oh, Gaudier! Gaudier's another thing. Gaudier is
marvellous."

It was Lowell's habit, whenever we met, to recall
to me the time before. A decade had elapsed between
our drive along the banks of the Charles River and
our second meeting in Bristol. "Do you realize," he
said on that occasion, "you are the same age now as I
was then?" As we sat in the Thames-side cafeteria, he
thought back to a charity reading we had both taken
part in the previous year at the Skinners' Hall, in the
London of Wren and the right worshipful city com-
panies. "Curious place," said Lowell; "you just
couldn't get a drink." I was puzzled, recalling the
wine there—its plentifulness had made me fear that
the Royal Hospital and Home for Incurables, on
whose behalf we were present, would benefit little
from our services. Why, even the waiters were
drunk—and had been audibly drinking behind the
scenes—by the time they came to serve the charity
dinner, so that boiled potatoes were rolling in all directions under the feet of the guests. "You just
couldn't get a drink." It was only afterward I realized that what he had meant was spirits. He had said
it with a curious, puzzled, tired little shake of the
head. Quite the opposite of that sudden kindling of
glance and face at his, "Gaudier is marvellous."

From the photograph of Gaudier at work on his
bust of Pound, one can see that he had previously en-

visaged the eyes as diamond-shaped lozenges. In changing these, together with a moustache which he had chalked in as possessing an upward curve, he not only removed a touch of melodrama of the kind which spoils the work of his older contemporary, Jacob Epstein, but realized a head worthy to look, and capable of looking, at the blaze of the Ligurian Sea through its narrowed slits. It had stood facing that sea from Rapallo, a little further up the coast from the spot we had set out for in 1951. It was the same sea that had killed Shelley. Across the bay from which he sailed to his death—"our" bay—a piano had once been ferried in a rowing boat for Frieda Lawrence to play on in the Lawrences' pink, four-roomed cottage at Fiascherino. The two Englishmen, Shelley and Lawrence, stand incongruously side by side in the mural painting within the Albergo delle Palme at Lerici.

I had gone to work as a kind of secretary at a villa, Gli Scafari, between Lerici and Fiascherino. Its owner was growing blind. Henry James had once described him—the first editor of the master's letters—as "of long limbs and candid countenance." Of an age now with James when he had said that, Percy Lubbock was still a tall man and had grown corpulent. The candid countenance was veiled, complicated to read because of the eyes that floated directionless in the heavy features. He had a Jamesian bulk and one fancied at the time—perhaps it was no more than a fancy—that its slack, unmuscular pendulousness stood in the same relation to James the physical man

as the style Lubbock had imitated to the master's
own. His manners were of an unfailing smoothness,
though a certain asperity  would occasionally pene-
trate his voice, as when he reflected on the quality of
the Berenson linen at I Tatti—"both the sheets and
the table napkins so much coarser than our own here
at Gli Scafari."

For the first three weeks we received nothing but
kindness. To begin with, our meetings with him were
few, since he was suffering from a cold and spent
most of the time in his bedroom. His friend, Lady
Dick-Lauder, present as a house guest, was affable and
absentmindedly good-natured, and in the evenings,
when we all met for dinner, there passed between the
two of them a certain amount of political badinage.
For he, as he described himself and as the regular arrival of the *New Statesman* bore witness, was "a bit of
a Bevanite," while she, with more consistency, recognized that for her better times had gone—she now
shared a house with her chauffeur—and had the
frankness to regret their passing. One evening we
realized that his teasing was directed at us. It was not
political, but one heard in it the old, ingrained,
slightly querulous asperity. He had been legislating
on the pronunciation of the English *a* as in *past* and
*castle,* insisting that it should be long also in *ants.*
Clearly he had not revisited the island for a long time,
for even the English aristocracy would hesitate to
lengthen the *a* of *ants.* But what he was evidently
indicating—as far, that is, as good manners permitted—was that our mildly Midland *a*'s sounded dis-

pleasing to him. But what of that? One could hardly feel wounded by a man who imagined *ants* should be pronounced *aunts*.

Two weeks later I received my dismissal. It was most mysterious. Lubbock had returned to Florence with Lady Dick-Lauder. The letter came from his stepdaughter, Iris Origo: he no longer wanted a secretary. Could one be dismissed for an accent? It hardly seemed plausible, but we could imagine no other cause for offense. We were penniless and homeless in a foreign country scarcely more than a month after our arrival. I saw myself back in England, once more teaching the recalcitrant children of Camden Town. However, thanks to the diplomacy and kindness of the Marchesa Origo, this didn't happen. We were removed to a *villino* adjoining the gardener's house and stayed there on a small allowance until the following May.

"Now do not forget," said Lubbock at his return, "you are still members of the same house party." This, too, was unintelligible, but he was as good as his word and would bring over his guests to see us.

The shock of dismissal, following on what seemed an escape from three years of teaching elementary school while trying to paint in the evenings, left me not only nonplussed but ill. I realized that I was worn out after three years of incessant work and fell all too easily into a state of increasing energylessness. The Italian doctor diagnosed heart strain. In the struggle back to normality I wrote most of the poems of *The Necklace* and had also begun visiting and drawing the sea caves at the end of that long rocky headland from which Gli Scafari took its name. Those sea caves and the islands visible beyond them have haunted my pictures ever since.

My books had found a home in the little room where the gardener's wife did the ironing for the villa—among them my treasured copy of the Sesame Books selection of Ezra Pound side by side with *The Pisan Cantos*. Both of these now spoke of a world which was close at hand:

> Lithe turning of water,
> > sinews of Poseidon,
> Black azure and hyaline,
> > glass wave over Tyro. . . .

This was the very sea and the light brought home now the exactness of that "glass wave" as one stood in the shadow of the sea caves and watched the forming and re-forming of the waters. I hadn't at the time associated "till the stone eyes look again seaward" with Gaudier's bust, of which I knew nothing. The phrase had run together in my mind with the memory of Homer's "grey-eyed Athena" and also with Pope's "And laughing Ceres reassume the land." The line of Pope had even detached itself from its grammatical context so that "reassume" had dropped its syntactical (though not its prophetic) connection with "Another age shall see the golden ear / Imbrown the slope. . . . / And Laughing Ceres reassume the land." In the remembered line, "reassume" was some unfathomable tense, a subjunctive abiding its full impli-

cation until perhaps those stone eyes should again
look seaward. The stone eyes were the eyes of a goddess, her statue and her temple restored to that height
where the olive groves swept upward from Fiascherino to La Serra, the village on the hill behind us.
You knew the way the goddess moved when you saw
the upright carriage of those women with bundles on
their heads walking down the stony *salita* between the
olives:

> . . . and from her manner of walking
> > as had Anchises
> till the shrine be again white with marble
> till the stone eyes look again seaward.

The poem received its counterpoint every day and the
scattered marble shone from the steps of the poorest
houses, cheap in that part of the country, with Car-
rara at no great distance. Gianfranco Contini speaks
slightingly of "the archaeological nature of Pound's
Italy." Trust an urban intellectual to miss the point. It
would be as foolish to label Pope's "laughing Ceres"
archaeological.

A phrase that had defeated me in *The Pisan Cantos,*
long before I had reached Italy and used to puzzle out
the book on the London tubes, read

> if they have not destroyed them
> > with Galla's rest, and . . .

Part of a list of destructions, its continuation unfinished. But who was Galla? And why "Galla's rest"?
Her remains or her repose or both? The answer ar-

rived unexpectedly. Our real life now faced away from the villa toward the gardener and his wife and through their daughter and son-in-law to the high village above us, La Serra. We had heard there the story that Lawrence had been told when he came to Fiascherino in 1913. *In tempi antichi* when pirates still used to harry the coast, the next village, Tellaro, its church fronting the sea, was saved from attack by an octopus. An octopus? *Sì, sì, un polpo.* Which had caught hold of the bell rope that had dropped its end down over the rocks. And so the village was woken up and rescued from the pirates who were about to raid it while everyone slept. In the version Lawrence heard, the pirates were missing and the people merely terrified by the inexplicable tolling of the bell.

We learned to walk up the *salita* to La Serra in pitch darkness to drink wine with friends—the family of the gardener's son-in-law. We would sit with tearful eyes in the smoke of a wood fire that used the room instead of the chimney for its flue. The wine was copious and one had to exercise a fearful control of the bladder—the Serresi had made of this a fine art—because there was no water closet, and to ask to use the family bucket would have been a breach of good manners and would no doubt have overtaxed the bucket. So one went out at last into the black night and deliciously released a hissing stream among the olive trees, and then blindly felt out with the feet the stones of the abrupt *salita* in the direction of Gli Scafari.

To Gli Scafari came various relatives of the gar-

dener's family to help with the olive harvest, rattling
down the olives with long canes. At Easter, Tina, the
gardener's wife, was due to visit her father and other
relations at Bagnara on the great plain behind Ravenna, and she invited us to go with her. We reached
there by train and bus. We descended from the bus in
the market square: the weather had remained extremely cold and the male population were still wear-
ing their winter cloaks. Fifty cloaked and hatted
figures turned instantaneously, or so it seemed, to
watch us in total silence as we crossed the square—
strangers and, what is more, foreigners. The front had
passed this way, and the village had been blown up
and now rebuilt. The question exercising those silent
men was: "What nationality are they?" A couple of
days later, as Brenda and I walked past a group of
youths, one of them stage-whispered to the others,
"He's a dirty German, but she's an Italian." "No,"
I said, facing them, "a dirty Englishman—*ingle-
saccio.*" But they weren't amused. However, no one
knifed me.

We were lodged at the house of an aging widow,
and slept in a large, warm bed—*un matrimoniale*—in a
large, cold room. The bed was heated by a warming
pan filled with hot ash. On the ample dresser stood a
single photograph of a young woman. It was slightly
unfocused and had turned brown. Buxom and evidently pretty-featured, she smiled out at the guests.
"Your daughter?" I asked the owner of the house.
"My daughter," she said. "She disappeared—*in tempo
di guerra.*" "Disappeared?" "One night armed men

came here and took her away. She has never returned.
I'm still waiting for her." "Armed men? You mean
the Germans?" "No, not the Germans. Partisans."

The bus to Ravenna left early. Stars were still out
and the North Italian plain with its leafless vine stocks
waited in dejection for the sun. In Ravenna the pud-
dles lay covered in a fine, wrinkling ice and as the
light came back it brought with it not warmth but an
aching clarity. We waited, penetrated by the intense
chill, for the doors of San Vitale to open, wedging
ourselves into the growing patches of sunlight. For
San Vitale we had come prepared, as for—later that
afternoon—Sant' Apollinare in Classe

Vieille usine désaffectée de Dieu

where the poet had assured us that we would still find

Dans ses pierres écroulantes la forme précise de Byzance.

What took us by surprise, after the hieratic splendors
of Justinian and Theodora glistening in mosaic
among the herons, ducks, and moorhens of a leafy
landscape, was the structure of brick immediately before San Vitale. The material had a simplicity and
roughness that, like adobe, could have encompassed
anything from a cowshed to a cathedral. The untidy,
frosted grass among which it stood gave it the appearance of something distinctly rural, almost reas-
suringly shabby. This exterior kept the secret of what
awaited within: the entire building was covered with
mosaic—Christ among his flock of sheep, dressed not
as a shepherd but as a beardless Roman soldier; the

apostles; Saint Lawrence and, above them against the
deep blue of arches and dome, mosaic stars, whose
tiny cubes of glass and stone glittered down as
sharply as the frosty stars under which we had taken
our departure from Bagnara that morning. The light
in there possessed an almost submarine phosphores-
cence and there seemed a touch of gold in it—

>    Di color d'oro, in che raggio traluce.

Its source came from windows sheeted with wafers of
alabaster: an illumination of glowing calm, the tem-
pered light of a not quite arrived Italian spring, the
sort of light the resurrecting dead might find easiest
to awake in before they looked out once more at the
full light of day. We had wandered almost by accident
into "Galla's rest" and under that vault of which
Louis Zukofsky was to write:

> . . . the eye can take in
>       gold, green and blue:
> The gold that shines
>       in the dark
> of Galla Placidia,
>       the gold in the
> Round vault rug of stone
>       that shows its
> pattern as well as the stars
>       my love might want on her floor. . . .

"Butterfly details to glint in his weightless structure,"
says Hugh Kenner; "alertly seen, acknowledged, left
in place, barely touched by being named, they pass

down a firefly page like clavichord notes, freighted by
no rhetoric of 'history.' " So lies Galla Placidia, or her
now emptied sarcophagus, the history she lived
through—captured by the Goths, married to their
king, exchanged for corn, regent of the western
empire—all subdued to this quiet luminosity, these
stars "like a covey of partridges," as Pound says in
another context. Once seen, the place was easily rec-
ognizable now, and, having read the great work in
unchronological order, I finally came upon:

> Gold fades in the gloom
> Under the blue-black roof, Placidia's. . . .

Archaeological? The experience of a diaphaneity that,
lost, can be recovered. Brick pierced by an alabaster
not merely marmoreal. Alabaster as a touchstone—
for light. A structure by no means weightless invaded
by its opposite or its complement. Brick and mosaic
suffering a sea change. *La cathédrale engloutie.* Not
quite: a stay to outlast barbarities. For after Galla
Placidia came Attila, burning down Italy in search of
her daughter, Honoria, who in a pique with her
lovers had offered herself to him.

On our return to the *villino,* Percy Lubbock
brought a guest to tea one spring afternoon, a guest
whose features I already knew from a photograph in
the Penguin edition of *Howard's End.* There, in glow-
eringly unbecoming close-up, with wide-winged
nostrils disapproving of some unidentified moral
aroma, the face reminded me of a Staffordshire
farmer I had known as a child and whose tart and

usually exact tongue I had always feared. Once he dressed me down for swearing when I said, "What a blooming day," and the sense of injustice I nursed over the years always stung once more whenever I caught sight of that expression on the face of E. M. Forster.

"I want you to show Morgan some of your paintings," said my ex-employer.

Forster's countenance was mild in comparison with that photograph.

"I have a question I wish to put to you," he said. "It will keep till after we have seen the pictures, but I mustn't forget it."

I showed the paintings one by one. Forster seemed to be bored. Perhaps it was the unasked question that took his mind off these images which he examined so patiently and so absently. Lubbock was in a benign mood. I never knew just how much he could still see, but he made a show of examining the pictures himself, murmuring to Forster, "I say, what a fancy he has—what a fancy," and showing all the enthusiasm that the novelist so clearly lacked. I was never to comprehend the mysterious footing on which our relationship stood, or failed to stand. I could no more read his intentions than those of the two benign Chinese figures that graced his library with impassive porcelain faces, their hands hidden under wide draperies.

Before Forster left, we came to his question: "You have just been to Ravenna, I understand? Now, there is something there I have never seen and have always wanted to see—the mausoleum of Galla Placidia. What's it like?"

"It's a Poundian building."

"And what exactly is a Poundian building?"

So, almost thirty years ago, I attempted to describe haltingly the effect of that lucid darkness just as I have done now. I could hear myself making my inadequate explanation, realizing, dawningly, in another part of my head, that the effect was one I had been half blindly stumbling toward in the scattered paintings that lay about the room, an effect it was to take another twenty years to begin to convey. Perhaps Forster had been right to be bored. I had a great way to go, and, if these scraps were only beginning to indicate the direction to me, what could they have possibly meant to him?

Before we left that May another meeting occurred—with the poet Paolo Bertolani. He was then just twenty. He had had no regular job since he left school as a boy, yet all his pennies had gone into buying books. One he lent me, *L'Antologia di Spoon River,* came into late fame in Italy, largely, I imagine, because Cesare Pavese had written about it during that phase of Italian culture when an imagined America—for Pavese and his friends had never been there—seemed to offer an alternative to an Italy "estranged, barbarized, calcified," as Pavese wrote, an alternative, that is, where the mind might come into possession of itself despite the prevailing culture of fascism. Thus, *The Spoon River Anthology* found its way to La Serra and still perhaps seemed to offer a literary model in a village where there was so much unarticulated life under one's windows—like the maid who, late in her pregnancy, aborted herself at the villa, flung her child from the cliff and continued to serve my ex-employer as if nothing had happened; or the cook who acquired a gun and tried to shoot the gardener; or the old, luxuriantly white-moustached peasant who offered a whole history of the modern world through his account of the growth and decline of *i baffi,* the moustache. He it was who, having found a dead eagle, carried it to the front of his house and spread out its wings against the wall. And when, as he said, his communist neighbors had asked what *that* was, he replied haughtily, "È l'aquila imperiale." "A chaste man," said Paolo. He never married and, having bought the land that had belonged to a local count, was known for the rest of his life as *il conte.* And there were those who *in tempo di guerra* had hidden in holes in the ground to avoid the conscription and now, like Paolo, were faced with the prospect of unemployment and looked to the communists—they had just won the elections hereabouts—to put things to rights.

Paolo showed me his poems—more human than political. I was struck by one phrase—"una statua di musica"—and I ventured to criticize another—"deliziosi cipressi." I could see that the two words made a fine sound, but wasn't sure that "deliziosi," even if it carried more voluptuous overtones than our "delightful," quite earned its passage there. Paolo frowned a little. "Curious," he said; "it's been much

admired by *una signorina* at Lerici, much admired."
"But put it," I said, "beside *una statua di musica* and
hear the difference." He wasn't quite convinced. The
English youth ventured out more boldly: "Not
Petrarch—Michelangelo, he's the man. See how he
twists the language to his own uses. He would never
say *deliziosi cipressi*. Petrarch might." There was a
deep, deep silence, a wholly uninterpretable silence, in
which (and this I did not learn for many years) Paolo
was cogitating on the ignorance of his English contemporary who imagined that Michelangelo wrote
poems, then deciding that *if* Michelangelo wrote
poems, and he, an Italian, did not know this fact, silence was the only possible answer until he came
upon some of them. Nor did either of us then realize
that in the next town, Sarzana, on the plain beneath
the hills where we were standing, another Italian
poet, Cavalcanti, had written in exile those lines that
Pound translated, "Because no hope is left me, Bal-
latetta, / Of return to Tuscany," and that Eliot had
transposed into a poem of his own, "Because I do not
hope to turn again." Sarzana. *Dove*—in good time—
*sta memoria*.

The final meeting with Paolo before our departure
took place on the beach. He was leaning against an
upturned boat and wore an immaculately white shirt
between a blue sky and a purple sea. In his hand he
carried a copy of Rimbaud in Italian—*Le illuminazioni*. Evidently he was travelling in the direction of
*una statua di musica*. Or so I thought. But his path lay
elsewhere. And it was not toward *i deliziosi cipressi*

either. I imagined he would surely leave Liguria for
Milan and on this assumption, venturing fifteen years
later into a Fiascherino the tourists had ruined beyond
repair and finding half our friends had gone as migrant workers to Germany, I failed to look for him at
La Serra. He had never left the place. His Spoon
River? Not exactly. His verse is more intricate than
that and less moralistic. But the discovery of American literature, which was largely the work of Pavese
and Vittorini, and which brought with it the desire
for an accord with reality into Italian writing, remained as decisive for Paolo's art as, in a different
way, the contact with America proved for my own.

Fifteen years ... We returned with our two
daughters, Justine and Juliet. We were in Siena—
"the most civil city in Europe," as the friend who
suggested it remarked. And so it is, its energies directed toward the yearly horse races for the banner of
the Virgin, the *palio,* and its violences also. Pound
had recalled the event in his Pisan captivity:

and down there they have been having their Palio
"Torre! Torre! Civetta!" ...
          and the parade and the carrocchio and the flag-play
and the tossing of the flags of the contrade

and he too had looked at the "four fat oxen" that pull
the *carrocchio*

having their arses wiped
and in general being tidied up to serve god under my window.

He also knew the wells of the city and walked the steep walk up from Fontebranda to the vast church of San Domenico where the black, shrunken head of Saint Catherine of Siena is preserved,

Narrow alabaster in sunlight, the windows of the cripta.

Had he experienced that other diaphaneity in the stones of Sant' Antimo, south of Siena, where blocks of—not alabaster, insisted the *custode,* but a local onyx—had been built into the walls to conduct a tawny, honied light into the nave of travertine? Onyx or alabaster, certainly not "that deep but dazzling darkness" of Galla's rest, but an intensity further along the scale of light conceived by the same sensibility which made possible

Di color d'oro, in che raggio traluce.

And, here, Dante is speaking of the paradisal stair—a Jacob's ladder of translucent solidity—which his own light could not follow out to its end. But, however far the monks of the abbey of Sant' Antimo had progressed along this stair, it soon vanished before them, and history, in the shape of the quarrels of ecclesiastic politics, transformed that place too into a

Vielle usine désaffectée de Dieu.

In that year, 1966, a number of coincidental forces had pointed us back to Italy—a parching thirst for the place, a return to its literature, and two new correspondents. I had read *Il gattopardo* by Giuseppe di

Lampedusa and went on to read the poems of his
cousin, Lucio Piccolo di Calanovella, poems of an en-
tropic history that can only consume, a history turning itself into fable where the Moorish predators of
Sicily became "la torma moresca dei venti," "the
Moorish band of the winds." I translated a number of
his poems and exchanged letters with this strange
man, an enthusiast for Hart Crane, who had, further,
read all English poetry and, as an investigator of the
occult, had been a correspondent of W. B. Yeats: "In
a lecture on myself," he wrote, "I have been called a
poet of the dead. Very well. The spirits are more
human than humans." An invitation came to visit
him at Capo d'Orlando which I always regret I was
never able to take up.

My second correspondent emerged after I had received through the post a small volume of poems, *Il
diapason.* The author was Mary de Rachewiltz, a name
which concealed from me for some time that she was
the daughter of Ezra Pound. Her letters displayed a
diffidence about her own poetry and, after publishing
a second book, *Di riflesso,* she recognized with an un-
usual certainty that she had come to the end of the
emotional need to write poems in Italian and produced, in English, that extraordinary book *Discretions,* the story of her life and of her relationship with
her father. Brunnenberg seemed a less exotically
daunting place to reach from Siena than Capo d'Orlando, so on our return journey we availed ourselves
of an invitation to stay there for a couple of nights.

As we drove through the Italian Tyrol, meeting

tanks, lorries, and armed men every few miles, we imagined maneuvers must be taking place. We were mistaken. The army was out to protect the Italian minority after recent bomb outrages on the part of the Austro-Germans who had succeeded in killing a policeman called Vogler. Once we realized the situation, we could explain why in Trento, when I had asked an Italian policeman the way, and in that language, he had seemed on the point of embracing me, and why, when north of Merano I continued to ask in Italian for the turning to Brunnenberg, I was given totally false directions.

Mary came out to meet us in a light-blue dress, preceded by her slim and handsome children, Patrizia and Sigifredo Walter Igor Raimondo, both in their teens. Patrizia had recently returned from a stay with her grandfather, who had been shocked at the shortness of her skirt and also by the fact that she had been permitted to go and see Brecht's *Dreigroschenoper*.

Below the castle, the cliff dropped sheer away and one imagined that bringing up children there must have presented similar hazards to the cliff dwellings of Mesa Verde, Colorado. But life at the castle seemed much like family life elsewhere and, though Boris de Rachewiltz was absent, there was a genial completeness in its atmosphere, one difference appearing in an inescapable awareness of the spiritual presence and history of Mary's father, and of the burden of deference due to him. We passed our stay in pleasant talk and in some local sight-seeing along the precipitous paths nearby—principally to Castel Ti-

rolo, once the seat of Margarita Maultasch, regent
of the Tyrol in the mid-fourteenth century, the Ugly
Duchess of Leon Feuchtwanger's novel and Lewis
Carroll's imaginings. The Italian attendant there also
appeared relieved when Mary addressed him in his
own language and he sighingly lamented the worsen-
ing situation and the lot of his fellow nationals. On
our walk back to Brunnenberg the subject of Lucio
Piccolo arose. Mary told the story of the visit two
Italian publishers had made to Capo d'Orlando. The
barone of Calanovella had received them, after their
fourteen-hour train journey, with an effusive wel-
come and a portion of ice cream.

Beside Mary's generosity, beside a certain insouciance—the typewriter she had given Juliet to play
with "had belonged to Mr. Pound"—there appeared
from time to time in that hint of a frown into which
her concentration gathered, something of the tension
with which a difficult destiny had strung her being.
"A cultural orphan," Donald Davie was to call her in
reviewing her memoir *Discretions;* for the language in
which she wrote that book was not the language she
had learned to speak first—nor was Italian. A foster-
child in the Tyrol, she had grown up using an Aus-
trian dialect. She was now the principessa, wife to
a descendant of the Longobard kings. She was also
Pound's daughter, and that, through war, through his
sequestration, and through the ultimate failure of the
attempt to make a home for him at Brunnenberg, had
left the deepest mark. "Do not take your father too
literally—or too seriously." These were the words of

Daniel Cory, Santayana's secretary and executor, who was also staying at the castle. His general air of mischievousness about Pound, the privilege of an old friend, served clearly as an attempt to take away the small, gathering frown from her eyes—the same frown that touches the face of Mary as a small girl on the cover photograph of her book. The presence beside her then, with tilted trilby, Bohemian cravat, and energetic beard, still looked down at her from Gaudier's profile on the wall at Brunnenberg.

Outside the window rose the Gaudier bust. The weather was misty. The peaks of the Ziel and Mut hovered invisible beyond the vines. Tourists trickled incessantly across the field path, a right of way for centuries, up to the castle gates. The gates had been placed there merely to prevent them from coagulating in the central courtyard. The bust seemed to attract to itself all the strength from the uncertain light. Whether one would *choose* to live with it . . . It asserted now, from its context within a family's history, the massive, male dominance of the image on which Gaudier had based it: Hoa-Haka-Nana-Ia, the giant Polynesian figure in the British Museum. "I have made a phallus of Ezra Pound," said Gaudier. Threatening progenitor, it loomed there starkly white, a single mass of thrust stone, the antithetical image to that side of Pound which responded to "Galla's rest," antithetical also to laughing Ceres.

I had been looking through the notebooks Gaudier kept when he was forming his style, notebooks full of figures evolved from Lautrec but simplified by the bold lines drawn by a sculptor's hand. They must have dated from his Bristol days. It was dark outside. As I got up to return to our own room, I heard a cry and a metallic crash. Brenda coming down the unlit stone stair of the castle, carrying child and typewriter, had missed her footing. The choice of which to let go was no choice at all, and Pound's typewriter had gone bouncing to the foot of the steps to end up there buckled and quivering.

The Pound of Gaudier's bust was unlike the Pound I eventually met. This meeting took place not at Brunnenberg, but at Spoleto in the following summer. Pound's hand felt cold to the touch. The hand of old age. It is strange to have met the innovators of one's time only when age had overtaken them. Except for Eliot—glimpsed at a London party, crossing the room with intent, beaked features, his movement unexpectedly predatory (or perhaps merely expressive of the concerted desire to escape as soon as possible), the large, butcher's hands clasped behind his back and the shoulders stooping forward into the trajectory of his intended flight. Pound's hand felt cold and, as one took it, returned no pressure. He seemed tired. It was evening. *Don Giovanni* would soon begin in the Teatro Nuovo at Spoleto and I had been introduced to him awkwardly across his companion, Olga Rudge. Mary had spoken to her mother of our visit to Brunnenberg, so conversation came easily. I enquired after Patrizia and Siegfried. "Siegfried?" she said, "One cannot possibly call anyone Siegfried at this date. It's the most absurd name imag-

inable. Why they gave it to Walter, I really can't understand." Walter was sanctified by Walther von der
Vogelweide. Siegfried carried the ineradicable Wag-
nerian connotation. Miss Rudge, in any case, had no
illusions that the romantic "Siegfried de Rachewiltz" would warrant suffering for in the great level-
ling down.

The first two acts of *Don Giovanni* followed, un-
varyingly stolid. The sets by Henry Moore were also
stolid—scarcely sets for *Don Giovanni,* simply sets
by Henry Moore. The statue of the commendatore in
the final act—and this was where one hoped the
sculptor's imagination would come into its own—
turned out to be a paltry, plaster thing and the singing
no better. During the interval I found myself, with
Octavio and Marie-José Paz, in the bar of the theater.
Suddenly Pound came in, Miss Rudge beside him.
Photographers leapt forward. Flashes exploded.
Pound looked confused, blinded, vulnerable. He
stopped blinking, shrunken in stature, unmistakably
weary. His pallid fragility darted its helplessness in
the same instant at Octavio and me, along with the
memory of the great energy that he had stood for in
both our minds. We, too, were made all at once vulnerable. Octavio slipped away to the far end of the
room, silently mastering his feelings. "Il est com-
plètement boulversé," said Marie-José.

Five minutes later, catching sight of Miss Rudge,
white-haired yet gaily volatile, eating pizza from a
paper napkin at the bar while Pound waited beside
her, one saw also the saddening disparity that a differ-

ence of not quite ten years will make to two people
who have grown old together. But, then, Pound had
been aged by more than just years.

After the 1967 Festival dei Due Mondi at Spoleto, I
saw Pound once more. This was in Siena in 1970.
Crossing the Piazza del Campo, I met Walter de
Rachewiltz, who was about to join his grandparents
at the open-air cafe at one corner. It was the year of
the Charles Manson trial, the American phrases oddly
disguised by the medium of the Italian newspapers.
The trial comes back to mind because Miss Rudge
explained that they had been that afternoon to see a
rehearsal of Mercadante's opera *Il reggente,* adding
that the characters in this piece of 1840s romanticism
seemed more like Manson's "family" than *her* idea of
royalty. Brenda, who had been shopping in the same
piazza, approached with the two girls, at which
Pound rose to his feet, waiting for the ladies to take
their seats before he resumed his own. He spoke only
when Miss Rudge prodded him into a response—
"Yes or no, Ezra?"—which would be followed by a
single syllable from him of decided weight and clarity. But that was all. He sat concentratedly engaged in
removing every particle of ice cream from the bottom
of his dish with a plastic spoon. Though once the
conversation among the rest of us had taken fire and
no one was looking at him, he began to examine each
face with minute scrupulousness, losing not a word as
he leaned forward, picking avidly at the skin on the
palm of his left hand. A day later, I saw him, possessed of all the energy he had seemed to lack at

Spoleto, climbing rapidly with springy steps the tax-
ing upward gradient of that same sloping piazza. In
the evening, he and Miss Rudge wandered past arm in
arm, lost in their thoughts, and did not recognize us
among the crowd of walkers: they were two old
people slowly taking the air of an Italian August
whose sultriness the afternoon's rain had freshened.

I told Walter, on our last day, that they had appeared very much at one, unperplexed by and perhaps
unconscious of the many walkers along the Banchi di
Sopra. With an admiring grandson's exaggeration he
replied, "He's like Oedipus at Colonus." "He has his
eyes still," I suggested. "His eyes," said Walter, "are
not good now. Olga reads to him. The usual piles of
books are sent to him." "So it's not worth burdening
him with yet another one?" "Well, he tries to keep
up, but probably not. He's eighty-five, you know." I
asked whether Pound had ever known the abbey of
Sant' Antimo, that so Poundian building. "Strange
that you should ask," answered Walter; "We went
there yesterday." We made our farewells, then Walter
paused and said, "By the way, have you heard?
Mauriac is dead."

A year before Pound's own death the publishing
house of Mondadori put out a new literary miscel-
lany, *Almanacco dello specchio*. It contained Cantos 90
and 116 translated by Mary de Rachewiltz, who
wrote: "Canto 116 can, up to the present moment, be
considered the end of the Cantos. The voice is now
almost a sigh, but the mind still shines out like a dol-
phin." One was in the company of other poet friends:

Octavio Paz, Vittorio Sereni, with whom I had long
corresponded, and—the realization burst on one out
of a twenty-year silence—Paolo Bertolani. Both of us
were represented by poems about the Ligurian coast
and, more particularly, Fiascherino—I by one composed there all those years ago, he by one telling of its
subsequent desecration. So he had continued to write,
and in a style that was brusque, compact, fluid. I sent
a letter and received in reply a book, a manuscript,
and his story of the intervening years.

His job was as rich in variety of human contact
as—and rather more unexpected than—that of
William Carlos Williams. He was a member of the
police force—*vigile urbano*. There had been difficult
years, years of depression, poems, part of a novel was
due in *Nuovi argomenti*.* He was married, with two
girls, and had never moved from La Serra. An article
clipped from a newspaper reported a prize for verse
that same year and carried a photograph. I did not
immediately recognize the face, though I recognized
the expression, a hard, almost pained concentration,
the two sharp vertical lines between the eyes nicked in
deep with shade. It was the expression he had worn
that day on the beach as he stared seaward, a copy of
*Le illuminazioni* in hand.

We exchanged letters—though Paolo is a reluctant
if excellent letter writer. He discovered from Vittorio
Sereni, who coincidentally owned a holiday house
nearby, that I had long ago written a poem called

*His remarkable book *Racconto della contea di Levante* appeared in
its complete form in 1979.

"Up at La Serra." This work was something of an
embarrassment to me, for in it I had tried to imagine
the life of a young poet "up at La Serra" who

> knew, at twenty
> all the deprivations such a place
> stored for the man
> who had no more to offer
> than a sheaf of verse
> in the style of Quasimodo. . . .

I wrote the poem at a time when I was experimenting
in the use of Williams's three-ply cadences. It was the
first of a series in which people are trapped by political or historic situations. Without La Serra—and
without Williams—I might not have got these poems
under way, so once more Italy and America had
combined for me. By the seventies, however, and by
the time I resumed contact with Paolo, I came to
wonder whether I had not been tactless in using
names—his name, in particular—and presumptuous,
even, in venturing to imagine what had been in his
mind in the 1950s. When, however, Paolo published a
new volume, *Incertezza dei bersagli,* in 1976, Vittorio
Sereni introduced it to an audience in Vicenza, in the
presence of the poet, by reading his own translation
of "Up at La Serra." Paolo's approval of that poem,
"a sociological picture" as Sereni called it, made me
feel that I could at least look him in the face. And this,
before long, I did.

In *Incertezza dei bersagli* there appears a poem enti-
tled "La casa di Charles"—the house, that is, where

we had met in 1952. It records the alterations undergone by that landscape "of a severe grace," and it
concludes:

If you return do not
return unless riding astride
a sea-bird's back from some spot
where even in flight the eye
can't seize on this scape that men
and the years have unshaped from the play that was life.

But his letters insisted, "You MUST come back." And:
"There are still here and there—especially at La Serra
and La Rocchetta—places that keep their old sub-
stance." "Here (among the alleys, off the roadways
invaded by *i prodotti Fiat*) there is a certain peace, an
ancient silence. The houses are still those of time gone
by with pots of basil in their narrow windows."

   Coming back after twenty-five years to La Serra, I
realized that Pound's choice of European exile and of
this particular country—for it was not merely a re-
gime he chose—had left its ponderable impression in
the literate Italian mind. For no sooner had I sat down
to drink the tea specially brewed for me by Sandro
Bencini, Paolo's engineer friend with whom I was to
stay, than our conversation turned to precisely that
theme—Pound's involvement in Italy. Our talk
wound its way to where, in England, it too frequently
begins—Pound's political culpability: "Why, when
he was part of the whole European effort toward
coherence," said Paolo, "he should ever have fallen
for—for *that* man." Paolo worked in a municipal

building from the era of Fascism—one that sported a
special balcony for speech making by "that man" or
his epigones. I advanced the usual explanations or half
explanations: the Great War, when others had lost
their equilibrium (Lawrence for example); the death
of Gaudier—part of the death of that new renaissance
of which he dreamed, the petering out of the great
energy that was vorticism. But what I'd wanted to
say was that I remembered a time, after the end of
"that man," when you could read on the walls of Italy
"Viva Stalin"—side by side, to be sure, with "Viva
Rita Hayworth." And I remembered also those in my
own country and the States who had trusted Stalin
and gone on to be judicious about Pound. Let him
that is without fault. . . . In all our attempts to be
judicious at his expense, we lack the generosity to
wonder why an American should have so desperately
thrown in his lot with Europe when he did. Donald
Davie, reviewing the memoir by Mary de Rachewiltz, puts us to shame when he reflects of both
Pound and Eliot: "[They] acknowledged in effect
that, since they had got sustenance from European
springs, it devolved upon them as a duty to declare
their allegiance when the European centre fell apart.
When we think what it meant to make such declara-
tions (what it meant for Pound and what it cost him),
the question whether they chose right is less significant than the fact that they chose at all."

Generosity declared itself when, a few days later,
in a remote village in the Appenines, I met the poet
Attilio Bertolucci (father of the filmmaker Bernardo

Bertolucci), an old enemy of "that man" and a diligent reader of literature in English. "It's all very well," he said, "for Contini to denigrate Pound's edition of Cavalcanti, but without Pound where would the revival of Cavalcanti be? What did the Italians *know* of Cavalcanti when Pound discovered him? Nothing. . . . And, now, I wonder if you would do me a favor? Would you be so kind as to read to me "Adlestrop" by your countryman Edward Thomas?"

One afternoon Vittorio Sereni drove up to La Serra from his house at Bocca di Magra, bringing with him the young Leopardi scholar Fernando Bandini and the critic Giansiro Ferrata. Over a bottle of excellent wine from grapes grown on the land that had belonged to *il conte,* Ferrata told us two stories of Pound from the 1930s, both of which were new to me. The first concerned a buffet luncheon Pound had provided for literary friends in Florence, and his mounting annoyance as he watched them helping themselves to the cuts of chicken, until he could bear it no longer and burst out, "It's me who paid for this little feast and there they are helping themselves to all the drumsticks." The second story recalled the meeting between Pound and the idealist philosopher Benedetto Croce. It had been difficult to arrange and, once arranged, the host was anxious about its outcome. Ferrata described the way the two great men approached each other, bowed, shook hands, transmitted signs of mutual approval and of how Pound pausingly, purringly, almost obsequiously began the conversation with: "You—you—are the author of the *Aesthetica?*

It's beautiful—beautiful . . . but—but it doesn't work." "Lei—lei—è l'autore dell' *Aesthetica?* È bella —bella . . . ma—ma non funziona"—"funziona" pronounced, as was Pound's way with certain Italian words, with a strong French accent: "ma non fongziona."

Toward the end of my time at La Serra, as we looked out beyond Gli Scafari towards San Terenzo, the place of Shelley's stay, Paolo suddenly said to me: "In all my years of living here, I never once, you know, actually saw Lubbock until after he'd died."

"After he'd died? You mean you saw his ghost down there among the pines?"

"Not exactly his ghost, but it felt strange enough. It was one day in summer—a hot, summer morning as clear as a mirror, all blues and greens, brilliant. That day, in my role as *vigile sanitario,* I had to go down to Fiascherino along with the health officer, the doctor who, because Lubbock's body was to be sent back to England, came to inject it with formalin as a preservative. It's a big injection—about a liter of liquid—in the region of the viscera, in the belly. Rather horrible. A kind of short-term mummification.

"We took the cliffside path past the *villino*—I'd never been there since that time I came to see you and forever afterwards marvelled at the way the English eat so very delicately, so very fastidiously. We got to the villa—well, you know the place: right above the sea, just a stone's throw from the beach. As soon as we entered the room where the body lay, what struck

me at once was the sheer mass of the dead man. So
enormous that he seemed to fill the entire place. Even
his face was enormous and very severe, with a decidedly contemptuous look, and it still expressed a
very exact sense of security, of command. Yet, despite all that, everything suddenly collapsed into absolute fragility as I felt the great needle—I say felt, because I'd turned my eyes away—start penetrating his
abdomen. And that feeling of fragility grew even
stronger as I stood staring out of the window across
the garden toward the sea, while the doctor was still
going on with his endless injection: I could hear the
unconcerned voices of morning bathers echoing up
from the beach below.

"There I stood, looking through the window into
the blaze of summer, when suddenly—very close,
almost as though by stretching out a hand I could
have touched them—I saw a couple of field mice leap-
ing from one palm to another, and those lines of
Montale from *La bufera* came into my mind: '. . . e il
volo da trapezio / dei topi familiari da una palma / all'
altra . . .' and I quoted them to the doctor—partly to
communicate with somebody, and partly to absolve
myself from that guilty literary thought coming at a
moment like this; partly, also, because I knew of his
keen interest in poetry. The reasons hardly added up.
And the sense of discontinuity brought on another
literary thought—Kafka—and the doctor murmured
something about life continuing nevertheless out
there despite the presence of this massive corpse, and
despite all the other corpses; and he went on about the

pure relativity of everything as he continued with his work. And the dead man, when you looked at him after that unforeseen intrusion of the everyday, and even of the banal, into the room and into *us,* the dead man was still enormous even in his fragility, although, as you might say, he no longer carried any weight, any significance. That was the first and only time I saw Lubbock."

With Lubbock's death, a last survival of James's Italy had gone too. For he, in his day, had married his American heiress, whom he had survived, to die in this villa of hers overlooking the sea that was Shelley's, Lawrence's, Pound's, Montale's, and now, for a given time, ours. When Paolo had finished speaking, we could hear beneath us, filtering upward from between the hacked olive groves and the sea, the constant burden of accompaniment of summer Fiats as they circulated past a Gli Scafari overshadowed by hotels, in search of parking space along the once narrow road where the only sound had been the klaxon of the bus passing at morning and at evening.

# Index